SCIENCE AND CULTURE SERIES

JOSEPH HUSSLEIN, S.J., Ph.D., GENERAL EDITOR

TRADITION AND PROGRESS

TRADITION
AND
PROGRESS

AND OTHER HISTORICAL
ESSAYS IN CULTURE,
RELIGION, AND POLITICS .

ROSS HOFFMAN

THE BRUCE PUBLISHING COMPANY
MILWAUKEE

To
Herbert Clifford Francis Bell
in friendship and admiration

PREFACE BY THE GENERAL EDITOR

IN A challenging series of chapters Professor Ross Hoffman pleads for a consideration of our important problems in the light of reason and experience. The need of recourse to tradition, thus expressed, has been recognized throughout the ages.

Tradition, as here conceived, implies in one precious word all those doctrines, principles, courtesies, and noble refinements of life which have been honored in the Christian past. Distinct from purely material progress, it includes, above all else, those things by which the human spirit can attain its full perfection. Without it man and society must inevitably be disillusioned. Though at the proudest height of their material prosperity, they may be deeply impoverished in spiritual values and ripe for their decline. Luxury enfeebles a nation, arouses bitterness, and begets strife. Ruin comes in the night. "Because thou sayest: I am rich and made wealthy, and have need of nothing: and knowest not that thou art wretched, and miserable, and poor, and blind, and naked."*

It is an upstart people that fails to honor the past. Its fate deserves to be inglorious. All the world's greatest work has depended on fidelity to tradition no less than on its own originality. Neither of these two conditions needs to exclude the other.

The tradition specifically in mind here is the memory of

---

* Apoc. 3:17.

that Christianized classical culture by which, throughout the long period of the Dark Ages followed by the highly artistic and intellectual Middle Ages, Europe was slowly built up into a society of nations. It is a culture which endured a thousand years. To forego the value of this tradition for our intellectual and spiritual life could be paralleled only, in the material order, by beginning over again our human development at the primitive stage of Mousterian man.

To refer to the Church as medieval, the author points out, is a serious mistake. It was the Hellenic-Roman culture which existed in the days of Christ. It was this culture which the Church Christianized, and so handed down in the West as a heritage to the Middle Ages. What is best in our own time has been derived from it. Its character remains impressed upon our civilization even where the soul has long ago departed and left but the outward form. But the Church herself is "supra-cultural," limited to no culture or civilization, no century, no race. East and West shall meet in her alone. Her sphere is spiritual.

Without foreshadowing too much the author's treatment, which I am here briefly summarizing, it will be helpful to indicate above all else the unity of theme observed throughout the wide variety of subjects dealt with in this volume. That theme is invariably the relation of tradition to progress. It is the goal never lost to sight whatever the nature of the problems discussed in the successive chapters: social, historical, educational, or political.

Characteristic of the violent extremes in modern thought, as opposed to the author's argument, is the attack launched against the study of history itself in certain American universities. The very discipline meant to promote well-informed thinking and to impress upon youth the value of a knowledge of past experience for guidance in present difficulties, is not merely ignored but systematically belittled. No one will question that history, especially in our own day, has its impressionistic school whose work is often little removed from fiction. But, on the other hand, to discard all historic literature because of the purposely subjective bent of such authors, or even, let us say, because of the animus of a Gibbon against Christianity and of Post-Reformation writers against the Catholic Church, is to be illogical. We must labor to remove the abuse and not take the easy road of attacking the legitimate use of what is in itself of utmost value. We cannot wisely dispense with tradition.

Marx and Engels, in launching on the world their Communist Manifesto, had a far shrewder insight into the value of history. But they, in turn, used it only to pervert it. Not guidance through the lessons of past experience was their purpose, but confirmation only of their preconceived philosophy of Historic Materialism, which has ever since remained the fundamental tenet of Socialist and Communist doctrine. It is the gruesome and authentic Procrustean bed into which all facts are made to fit — be they cut or stretched, as the case may demand.

And here we come to an underlying thought in this volume. It is the intrinsic impossibility for either ancient paganism or modern materialism to possess a Philosophy of History. For the Jew and the Christian alone was this attainable. Beginning with the initial promise of a Redeemer, it was possible for them to trace the entire march of mankind, in continuous progress, on to its consummation. In the Christian Faith this event is nothing less than the final completion of the Mystical Body of Christ. It is all one mighty harmony, like the blending of countless in-

struments into one sublime symphony of music, ending in
the triumphant finale of a culmination which leaves the
body breathless and the soul exalted to the seventh heaven.
Ye are gods!

Continuing, we see, in slow process, the building up of
the society of Christendom in Europe, and the great
Christianized classical tradition overcoming at long last the
survivals of pagan superstition. We see the deformation of
that tradition in the subsequent Jacobin heresy, viewed as
the predecessor of latter-day Socialism. Taking over the
Christian watchwords of "Freedom, Equality, and Fraternity," it misinterpreted their meaning, robbed them of all
their beauty, and ended in an orgy of license and bloodshed.
Freedom of the will, equality before God, and unity of
brotherly love in Christ is what the Church had taught
men. Searching still further, we see the inexorable logic of
the age-old tradition as applied in the Anglican Schism,
showing how Orthodox Faith cannot survive when sepa-
rated from obedience to Christ's Vicar on earth.

Then, chapter after chapter, we pursue the modern attempts to contravene the Christian tradition. First we have
the violence done to man's free will, by Capitalism and
Communism alike, in their prevention of that widely dis-
tributed private ownership which is the basis of true liberty.
Then, in the philosophy of the Totalitarian State but not
confined to it, we see ourselves confronted with the false
assumption that the citizen exists for the state and not the
state for the citizen. It is the pyramid placed upon its apex,
as Chesterton would say, instead of resting on its base.
Finally, in the more moderate methods of presumably
democratic governments, we behold a constantly greater
concentration of power, not seldom imperiling even the
most sacred and inherent rights of man.

Against all these excesses and uncompromisingly opposed to them, stands forth the Christianized classic tradition as the unfailing champion of popular rights. Long before, in an earlier age, those rights had been defended by a Suarez and a Bellarmine against what then was the world's dominant doctrine, the divine right of kings. Today the same battle must be carried on against the economic dictatorship of modern rationalistic Capital; against the offensive usurpation of indefeasible rights by a Nazi government; and lastly against the enslaving encroachments of a Red Sovietism, the monstrosity half capitalist and half communist, but all atheist.

Finally, let us be clear that tradition does not reject the advantages of any true material progress that mankind may make. It perfects and harmonizes it. Tradition is the indispensable condition of all real and enduring progress. It is the guiding spirit whose counsels men are free to neglect and whose voice they may refuse to hear, but only by ultimately paying the price of their own folly. For the wise it will be a cloud by day and a pillar of fire by night, a safe conduct on life's journey. To its full significance let the author introduce us.

Joseph Husslein, S.J., Ph.D.,
General Editor, Science and Culture Series

St. Louis University,
December 17, 1937.

A NOTE OF ACKNOWLEDGMENT

I wish to express my gratitude to the Editors of *The American Review, The Catholic World, The Sign,* and *Christendom* for the generous permission to include in this volume, and in somewhat modified form, nine of the following essays.

Ross Hoffman

New York
January, 1938

CONTENTS

1

TRADITION AND PROGRESS

THE word *tradition,* in the mouth of the average American, has a different or less comprehensive meaning than the sense in which it is used in this essay. Sometimes we employ the term loosely to mean some unverified tale out of the past, as if it were synonymous with legend; but more often we use it as Mr. Roosevelt did a few years ago when he announced his intention to break with tradition, meaning very sensibly that he would abandon methods of government action which no longer met public needs. Such use of the word is, of course, perfectly proper, but it does not exhaust the full meaning. For tradition designates not only established and inherited custom, but also the sum of truth, or knowledge, or doctrine, which human beings receive from their ancestors. All historical knowledge, the whole body of remembered experience and wisdom that is given over (*traditus*) by one generation to another, is tradition in the fullest sense, and it is so that I use the word here.

The reason why we Americans seldom employ this term save in its more restricted meanings is evident: We have had rather little sense of history. That is to say, we have carried in our consciousness small remembrance of any past more remote than a few centuries ago. Our history as a nation is but of yesterday and no monuments of great antiquity stand in the scene of our life to remind us as, say, the Romans are reminded of scores of antecedent generations. The beginnings of our national community took place upon a soil three thousand miles from our ancestral home, and coincided with the antihistorical Calvinistic and Cartesian revolutions in the mind and soul of Europe. Provincial America's renunciation of Europe synchronized with the emergence, in the old world, of the secularist conception of progress and the antitraditionalist spirit of the Enlightenment, which was to alienate several European generations from an intimate sense of their own past. Thus it was that we broke from Europe at the moment Europe itself was tearing up roots and clouding its historical memory; and a new physical environment conspired with our sectarian religion to effect for us a far greater breach with tradition than the old world was able to accomplish, even in its great revolutionary effort to make all things new; for we poured the new wine into new bottles. And to a certain extent we made the breach with a conscious purpose, deliberately turning our faces to the future and to the task of creating a fresh world, the while remembrance of our past grew dim. Not France of the *philosophes* and the Revolution, but our own new nation was to be the great test of that doctrine of progress which seized hold upon the eighteenth-century mind.

Now, by *progress* I mean precisely what that word has meant to the progressive historical theorists — to Saint-Pierre, Condorcet, Comte, Marx, and the others — ever since it became a common coin in the currency of western languages. It is a strictly secular conception: Man, through his practical reason and science, and through his natural merits, accomplishes a progress in his temporal life, achieving a condition of existence ever more satisfying to his natural desires, gaining greater liberty, security, and comfort, extending the subjugation of nature to serve his ends, increasing the community justice. The golden age of terrestrial life lies, therefore, not in Eden, nor in classical antiquity, nor in any mythical state of nature, but lies in the future awaiting the culmination of history. Such is the modern notion of progress, and we Americans have had it in varied form or measure since the birth of our nation. It came to us in part from the old world, but chiefly we derived it (and therefore as truth) from our own experience. Consciousness of the reality of progress was implanted in us by our achievements, and progressivism has remained in our national credo. The Civil War, which taught us that we, too, could come to ruin and disaster, did not shake it; and even the last quarter century, which has proved that we are not immune from maladies afflicting all the western world, has neither broken hopes for the future nor destroyed our intuitive confidence that historical life is inherently progressive.

And yet it is manifest that among us now, as throughout the West, doubts about progress have arisen. The world has been in serious trouble, and there comes an enormous literature of pessimism and criticism of the course of modern development. The spirit of reaction is abroad and a traditionalist insurrection issues forth. We have been aroused to a sense of peril, and as Mr. Austin Warren has said, "the sleepers have been awakened; the watchmen have ascended the walls." This is a sign of the continued vitality of our culture, but it is also an omen of gravely deepening social conflict; for it would not have appeared had western man not come again face to face with that most radical form of progressivism which aims not at any mere improvement of the existing order but at its destruction and the building in its place of a new kind of society. The normal, natural, and salutary opposition between innovation and conservative caution becomes increasingly a fundamental cultural conflict, forced on by persons who are not critics but enemies of tradition.

This kind of progressive has been powerful in the past, and he is powerful again today. A century ago he was Jacobin; he tends to be Communist today, even though he does not often profess openly the creed or wear the badge of that formidable sect. But he is recognizable by this mark of the mind: he conceives the whole of man's business in this world to be the promotion of temporal progress and the realization of some utopian social ideal. This is a simple atheistic doctrine that runs through a line of influential thinkers from Condorcet to Lenin and John Dewey; and it is, unfortunately, taken for granted today by the millions of simpletons (totally ignorant of western religion), whom the Left everywhere so facilely exploits.

Now, between this progressive and the man of tradition — the man, that is, who remembers and has learned from the past — there is a conflict without higher resolution; and it is the high issue of our age. Nor is the peril anywhere greater than in the American Republic. For our religion is weak, we know little of the tradition of Christendom, and the Left is reaching to exploit, for its own destructive end, our yet sturdy and well-founded faith in progress. That way lies its one hope of success.

2

Let us inquire briefly into the origin of the modern idea of progress. There is a widely held belief, characteristically Marxian and positivist, that this conception arose in the western mind as a reflex of the scientific and technological advancement of the seventeenth and eighteenth centuries. Man then found himself making progress and so came, as it were, to a realization of the fact. Mr. J. B. Bury, the historian of the idea of progress, found it first fully developed in the thought of the Abbé de Saint-Pierre, who was a characteristic representative of the first really modern generation of Europeans; that is, those who lived through the last quarter of the seventeenth and first quarter of the eighteenth century, were in touch with what went on at Paris, and first entertained the notion that the 'moderns' might be the peers or even the superiors of the 'ancients.' Professor Bury was entirely right; the idea came with the Enlightenment. But there was a very important point in this matter that Bury and a great many others have failed to see, and it is this: what occurred was not the birth of a new idea, but the degradation of an old one.

The history of the idea of progress is analogous to the history of the revolutionary gospel of liberty, equality, fraternity, and other eighteenth-century doctrine. M. Maritain has shown in his masterful essay on Rousseau that Jean Jacques' accomplishment was essentially to naturalize Christian morality; that is, to tear sublime truths loose from their roots in the supernatural order and compress them into the natural, thus disfiguring and perverting them. It was the instinct of the age to do precisely this: to naturalize, to secularize, and therefore to corrupt the grand sacred traditions of European civilization. And this is what the *philosophe* mentality did with the idea of progress. It degraded the Christian conception of the progressive spiritual redemption of mankind to a theory of human development in which the goal of historical progress is an earthly utopian society.

There took place a return of the ancient Epicurean idea of history, according to which man rose from the bestial state without supernatural aid, improved his condition by exercise of natural reason, developed the arts, built cities, and at length attained to the illuminating philosophy of Epicurus; which philosophy banishes fear of the mysterious and finally makes man happy. So said the ancient Epicureans, and so said the Marquis de Condorcet, whose faith in progress was as firm as his opinion that religion was invented when a knave encountered a fool. But there was one important difference between the old pagan concept of history and that held by the neo-Epicureans of the Enlightenment. The latter had also a vision of the future and therefore a 'philosophy of history,' in which the culmination of the historical process had not yet been reached, but lay ahead. And that is the reason why we may say that the Christian vision of the historical process was not so much discarded as degraded.

The fact should be plain from reflection on the inner and deeper currents of the historical stream along which we have come, for to perceive it one has only to ask how the idea of history as having significant direction could have entered the human mind. This is not an inference from nature, the life of which is rather repetitious than progressive. Nor is it an inference from man's experience of himself in a life of mere time and nature. No such idea is to be found in pagan or oriental antiquity, save of course

in the very significant instance of the Jews, who were
custodians of a sacred historical tradition and a prophetic
revelation of a great event to come. Greek speculation,
which achieved the highest flight of the pre-Christian
natural intelligence, attained to no philosophy of history
whatever. Plato's notion, fancifully held, was that history
proceeds through repetitious and apparently meaningless
cycles; and such a conception was current generally in the
classical age. "It may almost be described," wrote Bury, "as
the orthodox theory of cosmic time among the Greeks, and
it passed from them to the Romans." Nor can the mind
closed in nature and unillumined by revelation attain to
any other view of history than that it repeats, or at least
parallels itself, without hint of meaning, over and over
again.

Hence it was that in antiquity, although a sense of age
and weariness came upon society, the study of history was
not highly valued, and there was no looking back upon
a long perspective of remembered and meaningful historical life, but only to a vague yesterday fading quickly into
myth. It is true that patriotism such as that of Rome caused
men to prize their own great national traditions; but nobody
knew where man came from. He found himself existing
in nature with no remembrance of the morning of the
world; and so his background was only in nature, and he
did not conceive himself as the product of a historical
formation. Nor could there have come any change in this
unhistorical consciousness had not some unique event occurred, to pierce the closed repetitious cycle, illumine the
past, and affirm direction and goal in historical life.

Such an event at length occurred. It was the coming of
the historical Christ from out of the transcendent heaven,
to confirm the Jewish prophetic tradition and begin at last

a meaningful historical action: the redemption of mankind through progressive incorporation in His mystical body. This was the birth of the idea of progress, the revelation of the supernatural truth that mankind is marching through time to a consummation and destiny. It was, therefore, the cause of the growth of historical consciousness (so weak in Thucydides, the historian; so strong in St. Augustine, the theologian) which has been a distinguishing mark of the culture of the Christianized world. As Oswald Spengler shrewdly observed, "we men of Western Culture are, with our historical sense, an exception and not a rule. World-history is our world-picture, and not all mankind's." That is a statement of deep meaning, and if Spengler had probed and developed it fully he could have shown that it is only among men who have received the Christian gospel, with its revelation of human destiny, that a concept of meaningful historical progress, embracing universal mankind, has ever been manifest. The pagan world did not have it in the past and does not possess it today, for this sense of historical progress is in truth not precisely western but Christian; it is the distinctive mark of a mind once formed by the vision of the Redemption as a transcendental reality manifesting itself as a historical action in the life of the human race. No other sign has been given that the road of history leads anywhere at all.

Many, of course, will say this is not so. They will say, as, for example, the Marxist says, that the history of mankind has been closely analyzed and reason has disclosed the laws working within it. There has been found some principle of evolution, some inner logic or dialectic, which governs historical formation; so that although we cannot know the metaphysics of history (if indeed there be any such order of reality), we can know the nature of the historical process from within, and knowing this, perceive its logic and direction. Doubtless this is true. There is no need for discrediting the acute perceptions of thinkers such as Saint-Simon, Comte, Spencer, and Marx, for the complaint is not with what they saw but with their failure to see something more. They were groping for truth in history and did not fail of achieving some excellent results; but their minds were closed to spiritual reality and therefore to truths of history which are recognizable only when the mind is illumined by a fuller understanding of human nature. This was the reason why such thinkers, even when they knew well enough that the progressive vision of universal history originated in Christianity, failed to see that Christianity also made possible the progressive human advance, but for which the secularist notion of progress would not have occurred to the modern mind. Yet without doubt the Christian Faith worked exactly this result, and did so by implanting in man the idea of freedom and reforming his concept of his position in the world of nature.

By freedom I mean specifically the release of the mind from fatalism. For how could man have effected any kind of progress, that was really *his* progress, without a consciousness of freedom? How could he move or fancy himself moving, *of his volition,* toward a historical objective or consummation, as long as he felt himself to be either a mere instrument of a deity wholly external to him, or a pawn of the fates? It is true, of course, that long before the Christian dispensation men had asserted their wills in many notable undertakings, and the Greeks especially had affirmed a large measure of human autonomy; but the sense of tragedy, of man beating in vain against the prison doors of destiny, had soon matured. And the world of the spirit at the moment of our Lord's advent was

afflicted with despair and turning fatalist. Promethean man
had indeed denied the gods, but he was in bondage to
the fates, and as Mr. Chesterton once said, "the fates are
worse than deadly, they are dead." Everyone acquainted
with the spirit of antiquity in its maturity knows of this
pervading sense of despair, this failure of the will, this
brooding consciousness of fatality, reflected in the decline
and cataclysmic breakup of the classical pagan world.
How else could that mood have been dispelled than the
way in which it was dispelled? New energies, of course,
might have been poured into mankind by some despotic
god, like the god of Mahomet or Calvin, who seizes hold
upon men as the instruments of his omnipotent will.
There was much of this kind of religious phenomena in
that dying world, as there is much of it in our world today; for man has an instinct, ever manifest when he is
in despair, to lose himself and have his nothingness ab-
sorbed in some seeming great reality. But this is escape and
destruction, not the restoration of the worth of man and
of his freedom. Some persons fancy that Christianity, which
awakened in the saints an aspiration to be 'dissolved' in
God, had this unhappy action upon mankind; but it is not
true. The Christian God did not summon men to destroy
themselves for His glory, but called them to rebirth and
only bade them lose their lives that they might find them
anew, restored to infinite worth. The Christians addressed
their prayers to a God "who in creating human nature didst
marvelously ennoble it, and hast still more marvelously
renewed it," and they asked to be made "partakers of His
divinity who vouchsafed to become partaker of our humanity." These words from the Mass are the essence of that
Christian humanism which has inspired the highest flights
of the western spirit. It is rooted in the Incarnation, and it

exalts man as of infinite worth and dignity for the reason
that he is of the very substance of God. To bring men to
know their nature as such was the gospel that overcame
the fates and cut the bonds of spiritual slavery; there was
no other conceivable emancipation. For as Hegel never
tired of repeating, God alone is free because He obeys no
other will than His own, and man can only rise to a share
in the divine freedom by having part in the divine nature.
"Is it not written I said ye are gods?" It was these words
of our Lord that released man from the fatal destiny ruling
all merely natural existence and raised him again to king-
ship over the world of nature, which he was then to transfigure with his genius.

But not immediately, for something else was necessary
before man dared really face this kingdom and assert his
dominion over it. That was the conquest of fear: fear of
nature: the terror that had been inspired by its mysteries
and by the demons inhabiting it. The deepest discovery
of the Greeks, who had dared to look rationally upon
nature, had been that nature can cruelly deceive those who
put their trust in her. Classical naturalism had not led to
the discovery that nature is man's benevolent mother in
whose arms and at whose breast he may find abiding
nourishment, peace, and fulfillment; it had revealed instead the horrifying truth that nature — especially man's
own nature — can be a dreadful enemy, baring angry
teeth at man and breathing foulness upon him. The whole
experience of classical antiquity, indeed, can be summed
up in the discovery that the world of nature is not man's
permanent home, and that to treat it as such is the perversion of human life, for which the penalty is abandonment to the torture of demons. Nature is certainly not
our mother, for she does not treat us as sons; nor is she

even our sister, as I believe St. Francis poetically called her; rather is she our object and our task. It is our business to use her to certain ends, to solicit her gently, learning her ways, and to transfigure her after the manner of beings endowed with creative genius. That is the Christian doctrine respecting man and nature, and those who learned it were to find the demons gone. Then and only then did man enter to possess his kingdom. It is in no mere poetic or metaphorical sense that we say our Lord came to cast out demons; their expulsion was a main action of His Church in the world for more than ten centuries; and that action, of course, goes on. Not many, perhaps, have noted the deep and intimate spiritual connection between the gargoyle figuration on medieval cathedrals, symbolizing the demons expelled, and the rebirth of natural science in the great scholastic centuries. It was not only St. Francis who, as Chesterton so beautifully depicted him, announced the end of the long purgation and man's right to return to nature, but also St. Albert and the scholastic revival of science. A new formation of mankind had come: the men of Christendom, knowing their right position in nature, had been made, and the time was come for launching the great secular advance. The wonderful Renaissance centuries followed, opening the progressive era of science, technics, and in Francis Bacon's phrase, "the extension of man's empire over nature." Many men then unfortunately forgot how they had come to be the kind of men who could do such marvelous things, but they were, nonetheless, sons of Christendom, products of a historical formation that was of antecedent necessity for man's new mastery of his world.

Such are the deep truths, of religion, of freedom, of man in nature, that constitute the inner and most precious substance of western tradition. They were discovered through centuries of agonizing experience, and it is on their account that this experience is worth remembering. Were this not so, it might indeed be better to forget.

3

If there be truth in the foregoing statements, it follows irresistibly that the continued progressive development of our western culture depends upon the restoration and maintenance of our religion. If we fail in that, we are lost, and lost in the strictest sense of the word, for we shall forget not only where we are going but also the course whence we have come. Our past will lose meaning to us, and we therefore will not think it worth remembering. So will we, too, look back, like the pagans of antiquity, not to a long and meaningful past but only to a yesterday fading rapidly into myth.

Is this not in fact already the state of consciousness of millions of poor human beings in the ignorant and apostate parts of society? Consider, for example, what the term *Middle Ages* conjures up in the mind of the average newspaper reader, or even newspaper writer! To such people all historical bearings have been lost. As Bertrand Russell said not long ago, in historical sense "our age is the most parochial since Homer." We may fancy that we have attained the apex of intelligence and achievement, but perhaps most of us exist in a historical void, back of us myth and an act of blank forgetting, ahead we know not and apparently care not what.

Nor is there any escape from relapse into fatalism should our Christian tradition be lost, for no other doctrine of freedom has been or can be proclaimed. Modern atheistic man may yet exult for a time in progress because the world has not fallen to what is obvious ruin, but the sense of fate grows upon him. Suspicion spreads that we are in the clutch of forces beyond human control. More and more we are weighed down by a tyrannous sense of the inevitable, by the discouraging feeling that nothing much can be done against the trend of forces and events. What a depth of meaning is to be read in the seeming paradox that at the very moment man was achieving his greatest triumphs over nature, a sense of helplessness, despair, and loss of freedom began to creep upon him! It is barely half a century since the more advanced prophets of despair announced that man was not equal to his tasks, that he had failed and must give way for the coming of the superman; today a great part of the western world calls out for that monster to descend into our midst. Hence the deified leaders and dictators whom we hail as our masters. We are praying again to the gods for help, and not far ahead is the discovery that they can avail us nothing, for even the gods are ruled by the fates.

No sign of the times, however, is so menacing to the continuation of progress as the mounting fear of nature that is manifest today in the souls of men. I do not mean that the Rousseau gospel of benevolent nature is wholly dead, for indeed the mood that generates that folly has been notably present of recent years, especially among uprooted and fretful metropolitan intellectuals. Such people respond periodically to Baron Holbach's call to the deserter to trace back his 'wandering steps to Nature,' who will console him and drive from his heart the fears and evils that oppress him. No, we have by no means got rid of naturalism, which is one of the permanent temptations of mankind; but we are afflicted increasingly by the consequences that must ever result from behavior on the

principles of naturalism. The first is the discovery that
nature not only fails to satisfy the human spirit but instead
awakens new insatiable thirsts. And the second is the
frenzied determination to compel her to satisfy by feeding
furiously upon her like hunger-maddened slaves. So is
violence done to her; so comes perversion of right natural
ends, and even the loss of the knowledge that there are
laws of life; then the demons return. They are terrorizing
us again today, and one has only to consider modern man's
overpowering dread of disease, the spread of sex perversion,
and the fear of childbirth, to see that this is so. Let it
continue and the work of mastering and transfiguring
nature will end in another flight to the desert; for "this
sort goeth not out but by prayer and fasting." Beelzebub is
abroad, and only the God who frees man from bondage
to the merely natural, can drive the archfiend back to hell.
This is no mere figure of speech; no other metaphysical
truth is so well attested by human experience.

These, then, are the reasons why the atheist progressive
is not and never has been a genuine progressive. His sole
work for progress indeed has been to provoke our slumber-
ing minds, from time to time, to a renewed realization of
what are the necessary conditions of progress. In fact so
far is he from being a progressive that exactly the contrary
is true; he is a reactionary, and in the most objectionable
sense of a word that is his favorite epithet for men who
prize tradition; for he really urges that we go back to the
past by repeating its errors. Let us do, he proposes, what
the experience of western men has proved to be impossible;
let us, says he, be pagans again, not knowing that the ultimate lesson of paganism was the truth that he denies.

And the converse truth is, of course, that the only
genuine progressive is the man in whose consciousness

tradition lives: the man, that is, who learns and remembers what those who went before and formed him found to be true. It is no paradox to say in this sense that we cannot move forward to new things unless we cling tenaciously to past things; that tradition is not only not opposed to progress but is the necessary means for continuing it.

Nor is it less true that the traditionalist whose thought is fully Christian can never be that kind of timid and un-historically minded conservative who, lacking a vision of the ceaseless dynamism of historical life, would bid the world stand still or turn back upon its past. No, the Christian traditionalist must obey the maxim of St. Paul to prove all things and hold fast to what is good; which certainly means that the past is not to be worshiped, but only remembered; that it should enlighten us for the present day and that without hampering our freedom to do whatever commends itself, in the light of reason and experience, as a solution of human problems at this moment of history. Such a traditionalist will discern two necessary elements in the historical process, one conservative, the other creative. And so he cannot but say, with Nicholas Berdyaev, that "pure and abstract conservatism is unhistorical, since it claims that its function is to preserve what has already been accomplished. Such a view makes the comprehension of history impossible. On the other hand, a tie with the past and what is sacred in it is one with the creative dynamism of life; fidelity to the covenants of the past is fidelity to those of our ancestors' creative and dynamic life. A tie, therefore, with our ancestors, with our native land, with all that is sacred, is one with the creative and dynamic process which is addressing itself to the future, determining the fulfillment and creation of a new world and life, and effecting the union between the new world of the future and the old world of the past."[1]

To recover and conserve that tie with the past, to take hold again upon the truths of experience enshrined in the tradition of Christendom, that is the prime need of twentieth-century western man. We have been engaged in the mad and suicidal experiment of trying to maintain the civilization of the Christian West as if it had been created yesterday by a generation of atheists, and disaster not utopia lies ahead. We shall find out who we are and whence we came, or that disaster will not be averted.

---

[1] *The Meaning of History*, p. 39. Charles Scribner's Sons, New York.

2

MEDIEVALISM AND THE HISTORICAL MIND

I

AMONG the slanders spoken against the Church to the obscuring of its true nature is the often-heard statement that it is a characteristic medieval thing. Sometimes this is said with conscious contempt, the word *medieval* connoting barbarism and superstition; but it is also said, or at least implied, in many general histories written by non-Catholics, and that with such politeness as hardly to be recognized as slander. Yet slander it is, and damaging in the highest degree from its subtle suggestion that the Church is not relevant to the life of this historical moment, but is the relic of a past long dead.

Three main causes for this misconception may be set down. There is, first, the familiar Protestant opinion that the Reformation released the Christian religion from the dominion of tyrannical institutions the roots of which go back to the Roman Empire rather than to the primitive and Apostolic Church; from which viewpoint modern Catholicism appears as the continuation into the present of the Gospel arrested in development and imprisoned in a medieval institutional framework. The second cause is the assumptions of positivist sociology which treat all religions as details of culture patterns; from which it is deduced that Catholicism is an expression of the culture and social pattern of medieval Europe. Mr. Reinhold Niebuhr thus wrote recently of an intimate tie between Catholicism and agrarian feudalism, and such notions are commonly held by modern social theorists. The third cause, closely related to the second, is a heritage of historical romanticism, and this is the matter of special interest here.

At the beginning of the nineteenth century the peoples of Europe — notably the Germans — experienced a renewed national and historical consciousness. They underwent a traditionalist reaction against the Jacobin menace and were awakened to a new sense of the value of nationality, which is a concept that cannot be fully grasped unless historically. Hence there took place a new searching of the past for all the experiences of the much reverenced 'national soul,' nations rediscovered their medieval youth, idealized it and created new myths of a golden age. The medieval period which the neoclassicist eighteenth century had despised as Gothic was seen in a new light, and in a new mood, as a great creative age, heroic and of glamorous beauty. It was called an 'age of faith' and that faith had been Catholicism, which romanticists now associated primarily with the rediscovered medieval centuries. Many came to love again the old religion from which they had long been estranged, as men will love and hunger for the things of their youth; and hence many returned to it, often perhaps responding to a mood rather than assenting to a doctrine. The Faith indeed became again almost fashionable, although among reactionary conservatives there was possibly more admiration of Catholicism for being medieval than of the *Middle Ages* for being Catholic.

Now this romantic revival and the splendid literature that it inspired was without doubt an enrichment of the western mind and soul. It also gave some advantage for the Church to exploit, since the Catholic apologist was enabled now to defend the Church with new historical arguments; to show better, that is, how the influence of the Faith upon historic man had been to salvage, strengthen, and then to render him progressive and creative. Catholic conservatives such as Bonald, De Maistre, and Friedrich Schlegel were read by a generation cognizant of the lack of historical understanding in the *philosophe* mentality; and this was good. Nevertheless there was an undue condemnation of modern historical development, and this, together with an excessive idealization of the medieval past, conspired with the new positivist sociology to tie Catholicism to medieval culture; which is an illegitimate union.

And why? Because the Faith is supracultural, supernatural, transcendental, and hence cannot be bound of necessity with any culture or historic stage of culture. To conceive it as a specific classical, or medieval, or Latin, or European manifestation of the human spirit is to degrade and disfigure it, even as many modern Protestants have degraded their religion by linking it to the northern races. The various religious gropings and experiments of mankind may indeed be regarded properly enough as products of culture, which is purely natural, but the true religion is revelation from the world above nature. So that it would therefore be well if one never used so loose an expression as 'Catholic culture,' but spoke more precisely of Catholicized culture. For if, as Maritain has said, "Catholicism is to penetrate culture for the good of the world and the salvation of souls, it is not so that it shall be itself bound to one culture or another, or even to culture in general

and its various forms, otherwise than as a transcendent and
independent and vivifying force. . . . It forms civilization,
it is not formed by it. It feeds on the fruits of the earth,
but it is not of the earth, and it has an essential food which
is not a fruit of the earth."[1]

There is, however, one culture specially chosen among
'the fruits of the earth' upon which this supernatural reality
feeds. Our Lord chose to be born in the maturing period
of Hellenistic-Roman culture and to assimilate a great deal
of that culture (especially its ripest thought) into the
organic life of His Church. Doing so, He invested that
culture with a marvelous new life and apparently infinite
capacity for rejuvenation and growth. That culture
certainly did not die, as Spenglerians would have us believe, but was Christianized and revitalized. This would not
have been so, of course, had the new religion been a
complete denial of all the spiritual principles of classical
society; but the Faith was less a denial than a fulfillment,
and its action upon the classical world was not to destroy
but to assimilate and syncretize. Hence the Christianized
culture of antiquity persisted through the Dark Ages and
the Middle Ages, through the Renaissance and modern
times. It is alive today, however much transformed, and
we are of it; as we shall be for so long as our historical
tradition goes back to the Athenian and Roman republics,
to Plato, Aristotle, St. Paul, and St. Augustine, to the
Roman civil law and the roots of the Latin content of
our speech.

Medieval culture was, therefore, not a new culture but a
further stage in the life of the old culture. It was the
great achievement of medieval men that they were able,

---

[1] "Essay on Religion and Culture," in *Essays in Order*, p. 31. Quoted by
permission of the Macmillan Co., publishers.

after centuries of anarchy, forgetfulness, and ignorance, to make this culture flourish again and yield rich new fruits. Beginning with the deep spiritual reform exemplified in the Cluniac cloisters, there arose a fresh creative activity, a purging of the clerical order, a struggle to liberate the Church from the bondage of feudal tyranny, a reawakened sense of tradition and the recovery of hitherto forgotten elements of classical civilization, the revival of Roman law and of ancient philosophy and science, the reappearance of town life, of the guilds and other forms of free associational activity, the return of the republican idea. Feudalism and serfdom declined as Christian monarchy rose over baronial lawlessness, and small properties were created again. There was a growth of liberty, a great clarification of thought, and a rebirth of the arts. It was without doubt the most creative age in the history of Christendom; but it should be remembered that the generations then living were not only creating but restoring; that is, recovering a heritage from the past; for this splendid culture was the same culture which a few centuries earlier might seem to have died.

But there had not come the full development or perfection of that culture; nor was this a period in which that culture was completely civilized or Catholicized. There was still a vast ignorance of nature, which it is man's temporal work to transfigure with his practical reason and thus to create the civilized order that is required for the full growth of humanity. There was also an imperfect general consciousness of the whole sublime content of the Catholic Faith. Far too much coercion in matters of conscience (doubtless with adequate historical justice) existed in this age for us to call medieval society an order that had been wholly formed and informed by the spirit of

Christian freedom. Medieval history was a history of reason and true religion warring upon unreason and superstition, and a great deal of the latter remained unexpelled from the body of society.

Recently Father Philip Hughes, in the second volume of his admirable Church history, set forth the view — carefully qualified to be sure — that the medieval world was 'created' by the Church. This is a somewhat startling historical judgment, but we need not quarrel with it so long as it is not understood to imply that the Church was satisfied with its handiwork, or that this world was wholly patterned after Catholic ideals. But let us guard against claiming too much, lest we yield to the enemy a point that is not rightly his. We may certainly say that what was most reasonable and good in this society was there because the Church was there; and we may say that great victories were scored over barbarism, superstition, and other evils; but we cannot say that these were extinguished, since they triumphantly vindicated their presence and power by a great anti-Catholic revolution in the ensuing age of neopaganism, unreason, and heresy. One need thus but consider what issued historically from the medieval scene to realize its imperfections, which certainly were patent enough to the great Catholic humanists of the Renaissance, to whom the Church appeared as the custodian of the classical inheritance, not the Gothic.

But that deficiency of the Middle Ages which mainly concerns us here was the weakness of its historical sense. Karl Adam, with a fine insight, has pointed out that a major cause of the hard intolerance manifested in heresy persecutions was this unhistorical mentality. There were present, it is true, a sense of tradition and a perspective

upon the past, but the medieval mind was so much
occupied with problems of theology, dialectic, metaphysics,
and natural science that historical studies and speculation
upon the nature of the historical process were neglected.
Hence the "outlook was logical rather than psychological,"
and although the medieval man "rejoiced in the perception
of truth . . . he had little appreciation of the living conditions of soul by which this perception is reached. . . . That
epoch had no feeling for life as a flowing thing with its
own peculiar laws, no appreciation of history, whether
within us or without us." Neither human nature nor the
social order was understood as of genetic formation, in
ever continuous process of change and development. Even
in the greatest of scholastic thinkers this deficiency is to
be found. The world they contemplated was a finished
creation, fixed, determined, static, and therefore they
possessed a less mature historical intelligence than is to
be discerned in St. Ambrose or St. Augustine, who had
lived in the cataclysmic fourth and fifth centuries and
thus experienced in their souls the dynamism of historical
movement.

2

But precisely what do we mean by historical intelligence?
It is certainly not to be equated with intellectual possession
of a vast fund of detailed data concerning past events; it is
not historical erudition, nor any quality of mind necessarily
distinctive of learned students and professors of history.
There is an abundance of historical work revealing pro-
digious learning but little genuine historical mindedness.
Indeed the whole mass of eighteenth-century *philosophe*
history falls into this classification, and so does most of

the positivist historiography written in obedience to the canons of the graduate seminar. The scholarly description of a past age, as for example Voltaire's masterpiece on the age of Louis XIV, or learned narratives such as those of Gibbon and Macaulay, or the 'scientific' monographs done in the spirit of Ranke, do not necessarily exhibit the quality of thought we are here considering, although they are always, of course, the better for having it.

The test for the presence of this in any historical writer is whether he reveals a grasp upon the historical process as a whole and is able to discern the inner nature of events and the relations they bear to one another and to the whole of history. What, for example, was the breakdown of the Roman Empire? What precisely was the human activity constituting that catastrophe, and what position in the whole historical process does that catastrophe occupy? Ask the same questions of the Renaissance, the Reformation, the French Revolution, the World War, the rise of Communism and Fascism, etc., and see how this or that historical writer answers them. If he can relate these phenomena to the historical process; if he can discern their essence and inner logic, discover their roots and grasp their implications; if he understands the nature of the historical process not as a succession of events connected by a quasi-mechanical causation, but as a continuous activity of the human spirit; and if he can present us not with a post-mortem report upon the dead past but with an evocation through literary art of its living spirit; then we may say that here is the historical mind.

For that mind, I would insist, is not necessarily erudite in detailed knowledge of the past, but is in fact distinguished primarily by the ability to do two things as it contemplates the present. The first is to take the bearings

of today's position, to locate, as it were, the position of
the present moment in the course of historic time. The
historically minded man is in touch with universal tradition; he knows that he comes from somewhere; he has a
strong time sense and a share in the memory of his race,
which enables him to know that he is what he is and
where he is because of the course taken by a long spiritual process antecedent to his own formation. He may
have little time or inclination to make extended and
laborious journeys back over that road through time, in
order to inspect closely and with a depth of interest and
affection each step of the way; but he is never unaware
of the historical development that antedates him and has
formed both him and the civil order of which he finds
himself a part. That fact lives in his consciousness, and
therefore he always tends to see the acts and manifestations
of his own day against a background of age-long human
experience, which he respects because he senses its reality.
Wherefore does he always display a temper of sane conservatism, seeing well the proportions and relations of events
and never appearing as a mere rootless child of his age.

That, then, is one thing the historical mind can do:
remember in right perspective and grasp the present position in time. The second is that it can reach to an understanding of contemporary events that goes far beyond a
mere factual and external knowledge of their occurrence.
For the historical intelligence means above everything else
the ability to view the present historically and the having
of a right conception of human events as moments of ceaseless spiritual activity. It knows, therefore, that no political,
social, or economic arrangement can be understood unless
historically, and that there is no understanding of men,
of their opinions, morals, prejudices, and other peculiarities

unless these too are grasped with reference to how they came so to be. Consider, for example, the strife that rages in Spain at the moment of this writing. How will a truly historical mind approach that crisis in Spain's national life, in order to reach understanding of it? Will it be satisfied to apply the glib formulas of Rightist or Leftist journalism and conclude that this is a decisive conflict between a religious nation led by soldier-patriots and an atheist proletariat led by international conspirators against Catholicism and European civilization — or, if you like, corrupt and discredited reactionaries battling against Spain's progressive national development? These are clear and simple theories of Spain's present catastrophic moment; but they are fit only for simple and very unhistorical minds. They throw no light of understanding upon the concrete actuality of contemporary Spain. They take no account of the fact that a people of Catholic character can experience a revolutionary as well as a traditional mood. They do not explain how Communist and Anarchist doctrines penetrated Spanish minds; they consider neither whence these doctrines came, nor how minds were prepared to receive them. There is here no explanation of the decay of the Spanish monarchy and the resultant growth, over the past century, of the inordinate independence and power of the rich; nor is any account taken of the steady impoverishment, and therefore weakening, of religious institutions during the same period, and of the dislocation of ancient ways of life wrought by the comparatively recent and sudden advent of industrial capitalism into Spain. Those who mouth the formulas of contemporary ideological controversy and thus fancy themselves in touch with Spanish realities almost never reveal an understanding of the innumerable roots of this conflict that lie embedded in an irreversible past. But he who has sensed the actuality of history knows well that this situation in Spain, like every other social crisis past and present, has been compounded of an unmeasured series of human actions, each creating a new historical moment and all exhibiting great variation in motive and aspiration. So also does he know that whatever the future of Spain may hold it will not be determined by the political victory, today or tomorrow, of any ideology, but by the decisions which the people of Spain will make from moment to moment in that ceaseless spiritual activity which constitutes their history.

Such is the historical view of the social world, every arrangement in it appearing as a moment in a process that is ever yielding new and different arrangements. And in this view, we must not fail to mark also, the course of events is seen to be irreversible. Nothing that has been done can be undone, and no repetition is possible. No generation of men can live again their fathers' lives, no matter how faithfully they adhere to inherited maxims. There can be no retreat in time, no return to past actuality, no recovery of a moment that is gone; these things can no more be done than a man can live again, save in memory, the earlier years of his life. Forgotten truths can indeed be rediscovered and restored to dominion in a living world of the present, but nothing else can be raised from the grave of the past. Temptation to make this chimerical effort is the surest sign of wanting historical sense. Many romanticists of a century ago fancied this could or at least should be attempted; and there are 'medievalists' today who in all apparent seriousness propose that we turn back the clock. The same dream fancies plagued the people of the Middle Ages. Arnold of Brescia or Cola di Rienzi seeking to bring back the Roman

Republic, or Frederick Barbarossa acting as if he were
Justinian and the twelfth century were the sixth, these
were characteristic of an almost constant medieval effort
to pattern a present in accordance with a mental picture
of a past. And all such attempts were not only vain but
issued in disaster, as must ever be the result when men
lose touch with reality and seek what cannot be. Indeed
the great medieval order, so richly promising for the full
growth of the human spirit, was brought to ruin by two
reactionary efforts from the results of which the western
world still suffers. There was the attempt to restore classical
civilization, which issued in neopaganism, and the attempt
to restore primitive Christianity, which resulted in heresy
and revolt against reason. A similar kind of disaster was
wrought again by those unhistorical reactionaries whose
cult of classicism led them to fancy that ancient Rome
could be made to live again in the France of 1792. Doubtless the impulse for such reaction is one of the permanent
temptations of a human spirit which, happily, can remember and aspire. But surely it is an impulse to be curbed.
For there is no escape from the historical bonds that tie
every generation of men to the moment assigned them
by Providence.

3

We are thus led to dissociate Catholicism from medievalism not only because the Faith cannot be linked indissolubly to any age or culture, or because in the Catholic
tradition the classical inheritance is prized more than the
Gothic, but also because the integrally Catholic mind must
possess a historical sense that was barely existent in the

Middle Ages. I do not mean at all that medieval scholasticism was less Catholic than the radical historicism of our
day, nor that to be integrally Catholic in thought one must
dissolve a universe of entities into an absurd universe composed of nothing but processes and relations. But I do mean
that the scholastic vision of reality must be united with
the historical conception of society if our thought is to
conform harmoniously with the mind of the Church.

How historical is that mind, with its unbroken memory
that goes back to a divinely Personal beginning, and beyond
that even to the mystical first day — with its vision that
goes forward to the consummation of the world! The
Church indeed knows the nature of the historical process
better than any merely human mind knows it. It has
watched every kind of human thing begin and every kind
of human thing pass its last living moment and die. No
historic happening escapes place in this grand perspective
of all time and human experience; nor does any human
situation baffle this patient and tireless understanding. The
Church exhibits the historical mind to perfection, even
though it is true that at times her most representative sons
have reflected in their thought not this but other and
different aspects of her perfection.

But today there is not only great need for the Catholic
thinker to sharpen his historical intelligence, but little
excuse for his not doing so. Three dynamic centuries have
passed since the medieval order was torn to pieces, and our
world has been through a series of those cataclysmic crises
which awaken keen awareness of historical movement and
turn the mind to speculation upon that movement. The
part of the western world that was torn loose from the
Christian tradition by philosophism and atheism we may

reasonably expect to grow increasingly unhistorical and antihistorical; for it has turned from reality and its memory of the past grows dim. But the Catholic thinker, in touch with the mind that has not only endured but understood this turning away, ought on that account to be all the richer in historical insight and comprehension.

And the need is, of course, not only for the preservation of tradition, but for attack upon the contemporary problems that face us, urgently requiring the historical quality of mind. Many of these problems remain unsolved only because the thought applied to them has been neither concrete, nor practical, nor patient, nor cognizant of the fact that no ideal is ever realized unless those who labor for it know the art of the possible — that is, unless they know that in the historical process one can never do the work of tomorrow but only the tasks of today. The world has need of such close and careful thinking, and the Catholic mind (if it be integrally Catholic) should be able to provide it; which provision is, manifestly, of prime importance in twentieth-century apostolic action.

It goes without saying, however, that this will not be given by those who flee the present in pursuit of chimerical reactionary fancies, condemning the world of today to take refuge in imaginative dreams of the past, even of the great medieval past. For as Maritain has so finely said, those who do this remain "attached not to the eternal, but to fragments of the past, to moments of history immovably fixed and as it were embalmed in history, moments upon which we rest our heads to go to sleep; those who do so do not despise the world like the saints; they despise it like the ignorant and the arrogant; they do not think the world, they refuse it; they compromise divine truths with dying forms; and should they happen to possess a higher intelligence than the former of principles which are unchanging and the most acute perception of errors, aberrations and deficiencies of the present moment, their learning remains barren, incomplete and negativist, because a certain hardness of heart prevents them from 'knowing the works of men' and doing justice to the work of God in time and history."[2]

---

[2] *Op. cit.*, p. 52.

3

THE INSTRUMENTALIST ATTACK ON HISTORY

O N THE long front of the battle line that today rages so fiercely in our country between men of tradition and those who are minded (either witlessly or with full knowledge of what they are about) to cut us off still more from our roots, some of the most decisive fighting goes on in the sector of college education. A heavy fire of criticism has raked the colleges during the past quarter century, and not one of important note has escaped some measure of that fire. All have been assaulted in their traditional curriculum: all have seen their faculties locked in strife over various reforms which often represent not merely new methods but new educational purposes. And there is no doubt that it is the traditionalists who have had to give ground.

Nor is it to be doubted that the fact is for the most part to be deplored, since the chief general result has been the pushing aside of men who respect solid educational values by 'progressive' pragmatists bent on jettisoning things they lack the wits to understand or appreciate. A vast damage to sound college work has been done, and the only discernible compensating good is the now belated stirring of many conservative minds hitherto half asleep; in which fact lies at least some slight hope for positive counter-reform on sound conservative lines. Long has this been needed, for indeed the conservatives have only been forced into retreat because (as is so often the case with conservatives) they lay down on the task of conserving.

I refer to the fact that before the opening of the present era of experimentation the college was gradually ceasing to be what it should be and what it originally was; namely, a thing with a purpose. The American college had once a definite object, a specific reason for existence: preparing men for entry upon professional studies, especially studies for the clerical profession. It served that end; for that was it formed, and so was its nature determined. Hence the faculty prescribed almost wholly what studies the student should pursue. In that curriculum were reason and definiteness of aim; those who maintained it could defend it rationally by reference to that aim. And moreover, it may be said to have reflected the mind of a society that still respected reason and believed that college should drill and discipline the intellects of young men, thus teaching them to think, rather than 'adapt them to a changing world.'

There came during the past century, however, vast social changes in the country, and these were necessarily mirrored in its higher education. Religion declined, the while political democracy and industrial capitalism waxed strong, and with these came the power of the city, the decay of agrarian dominance, increased variety of economic occupations, and rising demand for specialized schooling. Many callings once considered mere trades were dignified as professions; and as our society, in its economic arrangement, became more functionalized and complex, in its intellectual culture it became more secular and antitraditional. All this sweeping change in American life took place under the reign of liberal individualist doctrines and the politics of laissez faire, the rightness of which seemed to our pragmatist minds to be proved by the growth of the nation, the rise of its material wealth, and its conquest and settlement of a continent.

Now this new society, like the older one it had succeeded, was mirrored in a changed college. The curriculum was invaded by new studies, notably modern languages, history, and the social sciences, which drew away the college from its old strict allegiance to the classical tradition. Also, under pressure of democratic demand, many higher institutions added whole new schools which not only competed with the liberal-arts college but showed a strong tendency to exert a shaping influence on its curriculum. Courses of study multiplied, rising in number like a tidal wave, until in our own times the thing got badly out of hand, especially in state institutions, which, like public secondary schools, had to yield before educator-politicians and the pressure of special interests.

Yet there was in all this no absolutely necessary engulfment of the liberal-arts college in educational chaos. An adjustment to meet the new age was possible through curricular changes involving no abandonment of clear and definite aim and reason for existence; namely, provision of an intellectual discipline suited to men and women as rational and moral beings. It was entirely possible, as it always is, to move with the times, neither dropping old and permanent values nor abandoning clearly conceived purposes. But unfortunately there was a general failure to effect positive reform, and the result was penetration of the college by those doctrines of individualism and laissez faire which were permeating our whole society. The sign of their arrival was the now much-derided elective system which, like Liberalism in its early stages, seemed at first to make for a healthy freedom and progress, but ultimately worked to destroy unity, order, and purpose, and delivered over the college to aimless drifting. Each faculty department showed an increasing disposition to emphasize its own special importance at the expense of the curriculum as a whole, and of course to resist efforts at centralized reform and co-ordination; in which situation lay a strong tendency for studies to become overspecialized, unrelated one to another, and irrelevant not only to life but to any rational end of college education. That has been, and is, the condition of the college which numerous experimenting reformers are attacking today. They want to overcome anarchy, irrelevance, and aimlessness, and close the divorce between related disciplines by a new integral co-ordination and purpose.

It was toward this end that a group of Columbia men in the social sciences, some fifteen years ago, began an interesting work. Although drawn from different departments, they combined to offer a single course of study directed upon the problems of industrial civilization. To use their own words, "they decided that the artificial boundaries separating the various social sciences made it difficult to bring all of these disciplines to bear at once upon the insistent problems of our times. They organized a course which is taught co-operatively by specialists drawn from many fields, and which considers issues such as law administration, price regulation, population, distribution — to take but a few of many — not as problems of sociology or history or government or economics, but as public questions calling for whatever aid knowledge has to offer." This course, admirably designed to apply related studies to specific and concrete social realities, has had, say these professors, notable and important results. "When economics had been taught *as* economics, and history *as* history, there had been little need to ask what broader purposes these disciplines should serve; and even had somebody raised the issue, there would have been few with the experience necessary to formulate a satisfactory answer. But when economics and history linked arms for the purpose of seeking out the insistent problems of industrialism and assessing the worth of the contribution to human betterment which each discipline might make, something new happened. Every one of the social sciences had to reconsider what it could offer to the common project and what lines its own future development should take. This has been a great gain, for it marks a transition from scholasticism to instrumentalism."

And yet another 'great gain' was this, that the teachers were led on "from a consideration of the function of each subject as part of a vast social-science project to an evaluation of the objectives of the project in general"; at which point they were face to face with the question so many conservative professors have been most reluctant to confront; namely, the question of what are the proper purposes of education, more particularly of college education, in present-day society. Some results of this encounter are set forth in a recent Columbia Press volume entitled *Redirecting Education,* which is of such commanding interest that it gives the provocation for this essay. Five monographs make up its content, and they are written by Professors Tugwell, Keyserling, Blaisdell, Cole, and McGoldrick. All have to do with teaching social science to undergraduates, and all propose reformed ways of doing this.

If the McGoldrick monograph be excepted (the author is a Catholic and his study is largely descriptive, cautious in tone, and comes to little more than a plea for less specialized textbooks and "a greater integration of work in recent history, social and political science"), there is a striking and easily recognized common denominator of thought in the views set forth in all these studies. This, I believe, is a fair statement of it: That the college must emerge from its aloof isolation in the life of contemporary society and be made to serve more efficaciously and more directly the needs of a changing world; that it must seek to equip students with the instrumental means of organizing and directing that changing world; that this objective is to be approached through the social sciences, and that it can only be reached by radical reform in the presentation of these; which reform consists in liberating them from the dominion of history and tradition, in short, making them 'present-minded.'

Now this is an admirable objective, but how do these reformers propose that we attain it? Here, they say, is this vast modern, largely collectivist society; it is a fact, whether we like it or not, and what is important for us to learn is not how it came to be or whether it should be, but how to make the best of it, how to keep it going, how to make it better serve our desires for 'the more abundant life.' The Great Society grew up, writes Professor Tugwell, "weed-fashion, unwanted, legislated against. But it colors our landscape, and we shall have to use it. . . . The persistence of this common nuisance we must make a virtue of; and we must do it wholeheartedly, pretending now that this was what we have always wanted."[1] The same note is struck again and again by the other contributors to the volume: here we are, and the main concern of the social

---

[1] Reprinted from Tugwell and Keyserling, *Redirecting Education* (p. 31), by permission of Columbia University Press.

sciences is not to find how we arrived or whence we came, but to show us the means of continuing on our way. Professor Keyserling has a very low opinion of history either as an aid in understanding the present or as a torch for lighting the way into the future; he wants students' minds kept working upon the contemporary scene, and tells us that "with growing faith in the efficacy of human effort there must be less reliance upon materials drawn from the past." Similarly, Professor Blaisdell holds strongly the opinion that the student should be introduced to the study of economics "by presenting the picture of a changing and moving society." The best that can be done, he believes, "is to orient teaching to the trends which have been recognized. Thus we either strengthen them or endeavor to modify them so as to achieve the kind of life we admire."[2] He, too, holds history in low esteem, and conceives the social sciences rather as means for the will to master society than as a light to the reason for understanding it.

Now the cause of this social-science revolt against the objective and historical study of the social process — which revolt is almost general in the American educational world today — is very plain, and we may find an excellent showing of it in these monographs. It is that belief in historical truth, or rather in the power of the mind to know historical truth, is growing weak; that subjectivist philosophy is storming the citadel of history. Scientific and objective history, built upon the critical study of documents and rational analysis of evidence (its strongest foundation), is mocked at widely today as an illusion of the nineteenth-century mind, a persistence of discredited scholastic and Cartesian thinking. Historical truth, it is said, cannot really

[2] *Ibid.*, pp. 153, 184.

be known; at best only a small portion of the facts of the past can be discovered and these may be variously interpreted; every age rewrites history, which is at best a probable approximation of truth, at worst a mere fiction agreed upon. Such skepticism permeates these monographs. Professor Tugwell says history "depends on what you have in mind," and is therefore "merely another instrument such as other intellectual references are, a kind of elaborate analogy having to do with something more important"; which something "just at this juncture is a deep apprehension concerning the availability to some hundred and twenty-five millions of Americans of what seem to be the instruments necessary to their progress."[3] Objectivity Tugwell believes to be 'largely myth,' and hence "for the time being we have had enough of studying history; we need projection and discussion of methods of attainment." So slight is Tugwell's respect for history that he actually proposes to prostitute it, to convert it into an instrumental means of social reform and management. Let us, says he, invent a historical myth in which we may say that our history had from its beginning a 'collectivistic seed' which has grown to be the Great Society. "Can we not indeed show," he asks, "how our history tended always to this end? The time is ripe for just such a conspiracy. Its mottoes could decorate our banners; it could clothe itself in a satisfactory glamour; it could serve for motive."

But Tugwell's dismissal of history as useless save as a myth-making for revolutionary ends is not the major attack on history to be found in these monographs. Formulation of that is the work of Professor Cole, and this is perhaps the more impressive for the fact that, unlike the other contributors, Cole is a historical specialist and is

[3] *Ibid.*, pp. 30, 31, 32.

really attempting here a defense of the value of history
for the several social sciences; but it is a defense that ends
in surrender. Cole argues reasonably enough for the genetic
approach to an understanding of contemporary society,
insisting rightly that we cannot really know the world of
today unless we learn through historical study how it came
to be as we find it; but he then goes on to suggest a reform
in teaching and studying history which reveals in him the
same antihistorical bias that is characteristic of Tugwell.
Once it is realized, he tells us, that history has as
its chief and fundamental object the attainment of an
understanding of the contemporary world, "it may be
found necessary to approach history by way of the present
rather than the past . . . to take some element or fact or
problem of the present and trace back its development as
far into the past as was necessary to give a clear understanding of the subject involved, and no further, then
return to the present, take another problem, and trace it
back." Such a change, Cole suggests, would "go far to
revitalize historical study," and would "avoid the danger
of teaching irrelevant facts for their own sake. It would
tie everything to the present and be a continual demonstration of the importance of history for an understanding of
the modern world, of the relevance of history to the actual
environment of the student, of the significance and meaning of historical change and historical processes. . . . No
longer would the object of history be hazy, the reasons for
studying it obscure."[4]

So would Professor Cole make history 'instrumental' after
the fashion of the reformed methods of presenting the social
sciences. We are to start with the present and work back-
ward, that is, teach history by finishing it first, and I think

---

[4] *Ibid.*, p. 211.

it ought to be obvious that this is a prescription not for
teaching history but sociology. For it is simply not true
to say that the object of historical study is to gain an
understanding *of the present.* That is indeed the ultimate
justification for studying history, as it is also for studying
nearly everything else, but it is certainly not the object of
studying history. That object, direct, clear, immediate, is
to gain understanding *not of the present but of the past,*
and when that object is not pursued one is not really studying history. It is just here that Professor Cole gets into
a kind of intellectual short circuit. He pleads justly for
knowledge of the past as throwing light upon the present,
and then proposes that history be studied in a way that
does not lead to any real grasp upon the past. For you
cannot get a proper picture of past times by merely searching them for an account of the origin and development of
what seems significant and important in the present. Much
that is most necessary for an adequate insight into the
life of the past is not to be had from that approach;
whence it follows that since the past is not understood
neither is the present. Such a short cut through sociology
implies, moreover, the loss of many enlightening comparisons between one age and another; which comparisons
are of indispensable aid to students in developing the
ability to criticize intelligently their own times and
social environment.

It is plain indeed that Professor Cole, far from making
a sound defense of history, betrays it into the hands of its
enemies. And the reason he has done this is equally evident.
It is that, like the other contributors to the volume, he
simply does not believe much in history. For him, too,
objectivity is myth. "The ordinary historical fact," he writes,
"is, indeed, a subjective judgment on the part of the histo-

rian rather than an objective record of something which occurred in the past. If the status of a single historical fact is somewhat dubious, how much more so is the connection between any two facts. Should the historian strive for utter objectivity, his work would be composed of a disconnected series of bare statements strung together only by temporal or spatial relationship — after this, that; near this, something else."[5] In follows, then, in Cole's judgment, that all history is of rather shaky and dubious veracity, and he bids us recognize that the writing of it "is a subjective process" (one wonders who would deny this!). "Further, the historian must have certain criteria in the light of which he may select, order, and interpret his facts. These criteria will be the ideas of the historian as to the importance, relation, and meaning of the facts. The ideas may have some connection with objective reality, then again they may not."[6] This being so (as it undoubtedly is), Professor Cole asks whose history is true, and replies that we can never know, that we cannot actually get at historical truth at all; or at least, if we do we can never be certain of it. This is substantially what was said by Tugwell who values history as instrumental for myth-making. Cole falls back upon much the same position, saying that all this "does not reduce the value of history" because we may take refuge from despair of knowing the past with certainty in the 'As If' philosophy of Vaihinger; who "has demonstrated clearly that the use of fictions, myths, unfounded figures of speech, and so on leads in many cases to perfectly correct results." So that although our history may be false, we can pretend that it is true and teach it anyway!

---

[5] *Ibid.*, pp. 212, 213.
[6] *Ibid.*, p. 214.

Such is the defense, and doubtless the best defense, that can be made of history today by men who have ceased to believe in reason, in the capacity of the rational intellect to know with certainty. For that, manifestly, is fundamental in all this revolt against the affirmation that the past can be known. What you have are men saying that the human reason cannot take certain hold upon truth, that rational analysis working upon evidence cannot draw out truth from it. This attack on historical objectivity is neither more nor less than a new undermining of the foundations of knowledge by the currents of skepticism set in motion in the western mind two centuries ago. And wide is its acid action among the new generation of philosopher-historians who have arisen to confound and dismay the older generation that was schooled in the Ranke tradition, eschewed all metaphysics, and conceived history as a problem in positivist science. Let this new doctrine win full sway, let it conquer the social sciences and go on (as indeed it is) to make over all college studies, and we shall see the end of anything properly called the study and teaching of history in academic institutions.

Toward that end these antihistorical instrumentalists propose to lead by giving us a new kind of education, and if they succeed, we are going to have a new and yet more radical break from tradition, a further tearing up of roots, a further loss of memory whence we sprang. Three centuries ago the mind of the West, captivated by the Cartesian philosophy, made the last great breach with tradition. Confidently affirming the full sufficiency and absolute sovereignty of human reason, it soared aloft on the magnificent adventure of flying through the skies of rational science to the very frontiers of reality. Today it completes the downward curve of the arc that was so inscribed, returning to earth with the news that reason has failed, that man cannot really know anything with certainty, not even now his own past. Once that past was disavowed in the name of reason, and now we are bidden to disavow it again in the name of unreason. Of such is this new reform.

4

MARXIST HISTORY AND LIBERALISM

ALTHOUGH it is true that our contemporary Communists often seem to be mere epigones of the great eighteenth-century revolutionaries — often appear, indeed, as but the inheritors of a tradition now stripped of its one-time nobility and moral grandeur — there is one important respect in which the Communist mind of today excels the revolutionary mind of a century and a half ago. And it is this: the Communist intellectual whose mind has been formed by Marx, Engels, and Lenin has a better historic sense, that is, a greater respect for the past and a clearer concept of its concrete reality than had, say, Condorcet or Rousseau. Full credit for this merit often is withheld from Communist thinkers because of their hostility to certain traditions and their ideal vision of a world brought to peace and order without religion, or to say more accurately, without that Christian religion which informed our western culture with its unique historic sense; that is, an awareness of human origins, a perception of direction in the march of events, a sense of historical logic, and a powerful cementing and organic bond between present and past generations.

Yet it should be obvious that Marxian sociology is profoundly historical in its character, that it is based irremovably on a certain theory of history which professes to comprehend the whole recorded past. The real Marxist is no utopian dreamer conceiving the advent of the New Jerusalem as a possible event of tomorrow, could an irrational world but be won to reason. He is, on the contrary, a historical philosopher contemplating the processes of social evolution, ever studying their trend with an eye to opportunity for the intervention of a revolutionary will, taking realistic account, as it were, of the historical justice of the moment. History he conceives as a progress, rather mechanistic than organic to be sure, but not, as Condorcet imagined, a progress realized by successive mysterious leaps of human virtue and reason. For the Marxist of today has enriched the eighteenth-century idea of progress with a vast quantity of additional factual data and with the nineteenth- and twentieth-century concepts of evolution and historical relativity. This is the reason why he is commonly able to discern no less than the positivist historian concerned only with the concrete actuality of the past — the emptiness of the old 'philosophies of history'; to see, that is, how these were imposed by metaphysics upon history, rather than elicited from it by careful and objective study of the documented past.

It is true that the Marxist makes exception here for his own philosophy of history, believing it to be verified by the facts, and he therefore stands apart from thinkers who reject the very possibility of a philosophy of history. It is also true that this exception is not warranted, since the Marxian historical doctrine, no less than that of Comte and Hegel, lies open to the accusation of being a transcendental search for the causation and end of the historical process: a search, that is, for what the human mind, from its nature and constitution, is unable to discover — save,

of course, it be illumined by transcendental revelation.
There being no Marxist epistemology, the disciples of Marx
who profess to know the philosophy of history do not know
how this is possible: nor do they ask, but simply evade the
question by denying the existence of metaphysical reality.
But to ignore what is logically necessary is not to get rid
of it. Croce has written wittily of Marx 'at his work and
at his prayers,' and it must be remembered that this
German Jew, for all his hard and painful fact-gathering,
was not a strict social scientist humbly soliciting the meaning of data ascertained; rather was he primarily a man
with a faith, a revolutionist bent on establishing a new
social order. History was moving toward that end, so he
believed, but his belief derived less from historical study
than from the philosophic assumptions which he brought
to that study; and the same is true of his disciples.

Nevertheless, it is important to recognize that Marx
turned away (not so much from despair, I suspect, as from
hatred) from all metaphysics and mystery; that he would
follow no line of thought that might lead to religion, and
that, leaving all such momentous questions, he riveted his
attention upon the social process, seeking to discover (and
by a truly scientific method) exactly what took place when
one historical situation was succeeded by another. Therein
one may find the reason for the genuine richness of his
thought and its value for historical study. For what he did
was essentially this: he set up a hypothesis, the materialistic
interpretation of history, and sought by an elaborate inquiry
to show this as true. It led him, and also both his disciples
and opponents, to extensive new investigations of the past;
it provoked questions and problems that had not previously
arisen or been noticed; it broadened and intensified research
into the whole history of human culture, bringing forth,

as every new scientific hypothesis will bring, fresh studies, and placing neglected matters under the focus of the mind. But the special point for emphasis here is this, that all genuine Marxians have recognized an obligation to leave no phenomenon of history, no event, no sequence or relationship, unaccounted for in their social-historical theory. Confident in their dogmas of dialectic materialism and the determination of the social process by the relations of economic production, they have dared to confront the whole human past, scrutinize it closely, and that without neglecting or shrinking from any part of it, but claiming all of it and arranging all of it in a comprehensive pattern.

Hence it is that no genuine Marxist, however strong his hatred of religion, would neglect to give important treatment to spiritual factors in history. Indeed the Marxist is conscious of a special obligation to deal with these in such fashion as to show them to be a reflex of the social-economic arrangement. Thought, religion, the various manifestations of the spirit, all this he is far from ignoring or sweeping aside as unreal. The power of ideas, once they have arisen out of a given social order, he knows to be very great, and he is in constant battle with them. It is not the Marxist but the Liberal mind that produces the numerous books of modern history in which the existence of a spiritual tradition in western civilization is almost totally ignored. After all, men who affirm a strict doctrine, who reprove and punish heretics, who make the fight upon bourgeois mentality and the Christian religion a supreme issue of the day, will hardly be the ones to miss the importance of spiritual forces in history.

It is just here that one touches the reason why the Marxian mind, in its historical sense, not only is superior to the rationalist mind of the eighteenth century, but excels also the later positivist mind as expressed in nineteenth-century historiography. It asks more questions, it searches harder for relationships, and it demands analysis of much which Ranke and his disciples simply ignored. Nowhere have I found better illustration of this than in Professor Laski's recent volume, *The Rise of European Liberalism*. This distinguished Laborite intellectual has now placed himself in nearly complete allegiance to Marxian thought, and his book is a genuine masterpiece, easily taking first place among all the studies of the genesis, development, and implications of liberalism, the history of which is certainly the central theme of modern history. The fact that the book is permeated by mistaken philosophy and a spirit that cannot fail to arouse opposition from Christian and traditionalist minds hardly detracts at all from its value as a work of luminous historical insight and sound and rich learning. For Laski not only has succeeded in defining clearly what in essence Liberalism has been, and in discovering its origins, but also has traced out in masterful manner the whole assault, on every front, which it has made upon the traditional structure of western society. The history of Liberalism as doctrine and morality, acting like an acid upon social Christendom, is admirably set forth and that without any failure to do justice to the conservative-traditionalist mind of the past five centuries. No phase of the momentous experiment in absolute individualist autonomy has been neglected, and all is woven skillfully together as the history of one great phenomenon of post-medieval culture. We have here a most thoughtful and informing book, and its high excellence derives in great measure from the fact that the author is able, at the very beginning of his essay, to isolate the germ of the Liberal

disease and thereafter to keep his eye riveted continuously
upon it.

What is this germ? And when appeared the first manifestations of Liberalism? Not with the Protestant Revolution; Laski is far too shrewd to fancy (as I fear many
critics of Liberalism still believe) that it issued from
Protestantism. Without doubt there was a Protestant contribution to its growth, and the severance from papal obedience which broke the chains of authority enabled the
Liberal movement ultimately to win its way. But the
origins of Liberalism are in the Renaissance release of
appetites, not in the Protestant reform of religion. "By the
end of the fifteenth century," writes Mr. Laski, "the capitalist spirit began to attain a predominant hold over men's
minds. What does this imply? That the pursuit of wealth
for its own sake became the chief motive of human activity. Whereas in the Middle Ages the idea of acquiring
wealth was limited by a body of moral rules imposed under
the sanction of religious authority, after 1500 those rules,
and the institutions, habits, and ideas to which they had
given birth, were no longer deemed adequate. They were
evaded, criticized, abandoned, because it was felt that they
interfered with the exploitation of the means of production. New conceptions were needed to legitimize the new
potentialities of wealth that man had discovered little by
little in preceding ages. The liberal doctrine is the philosophic justification of the new practices."

In writing this Mr. Laski has put his finger on the very
essence of the Liberal movement, and it does not escape
from his touch at any time, but ever appears clearly before
him as the method and doctrine devised to enfranchise and
rationalize the unrestricted appetites of capitalist individual-

ism. "A social conception of wealth gives place to an individualist conception. The idea of a divine sanction for the rules of behavior is gradually replaced by a utilitarian sanction. And the principle of utility is no longer determined by reference to social good. Its meaning is taken from the desire to satisfy individual want. . . . Once this attitude begins to obtain hold over men's minds, it develops a revolutionary power. It . . . implies a society which is dynamic and anti-traditional because, since the desire for wealth is endless it must continuously seek experiment and novelty." For as Mr. Laski remarks in another connection, "the inner idea of capitalism is inherently a philosophy of life. Those who accept it do not need extra-capitalist sources to validate their activities. Their search for wealth as individuals colors and shapes their attitude to every department of behavior. Unless this had been the case, capitalism could not have achieved the revolution it effected. There was no sphere of life in which it did not encounter norms of conduct resistant to its spirit. Without exception it transformed them, or sought to do so. . . . The whole ethos of capitalism, in a word, is its effort to free the owner of the instruments of production from the need to obey rules which inhibit his full exploitation of them. The rise of Liberalism is the rise of a doctrine which seeks to justify the operation of that ethos."

Now, in presenting these quoted words wherein Mr. Laski so admirably pares Liberalism down to its essential core, I am far from inferring that his volume as a whole is without serious defects. These are present and even conspicuous; and they are precisely the defects one always finds in Marxist history. There is, for example, Mr. Laski's continuous and wholly unsuccessful effort to relate every manifestation of the liberal development to the interests and activities of the so-called middle class — as if only the members of this class were infected with the capitalist spirit, and only these chafed against the restraints upon economic appetites! Again, his thought is clouded on a point of such capital importance as to be vital to the whole Marx-Laski theory of history. In words that I have quoted above he writes of the *capitalist spirit taking hold upon men's minds,* implying plainly that some change of a moral and spiritual character was taking place in medieval Christendom, causing men to be less resistant to the temptations of greedy appetite. But instead of locating causation of unbridled capitalism in the spiritual order, where obviously it is to be found, he writes this: "If we ask why the capitalist spirit triumphed, the answer, surely, is the sufficient one that within the confines of the older system the potentialities of production could no longer be exploited." Now I think we must insist that this answer is very far from sufficient, that it is in fact a mere begging of the question. For it is nothing short of absurd to say that men who regard economic appetites as properly governable by moral authority will then deny that authority if it interferes with the satisfaction of appetites — unless of course they have decided to change their morals. But such absurdity is unavoidable for philosophers who fancy that morality is determined by economics, since the truth is the other way round.

One may also complain with justice against Mr. Laski on a few other counts, as for example, his failure to appreciate how much strength Liberalism derived from its continuous exploitation of traditional moral values; which failure is due to the author's determination to make of the movement a purely class manifestation, reflecting the interests and appetites of the bourgeoisie. But all this may be passed over lightly and even forgiven in a work which analyzes and delineates so clearly the evolution of the Liberal movement — obedient always to the logic of its inner nature — to the point reached in the moral and social anarchy of our day. One may dissent sharply from Mr. Laski's judgment of future probabilities and of the way we must take if moral and economic order are to be restored, but there is no denying that he has helped greatly to illuminate the way that we followed to the present pass.

5

A PESSIMIST PHILOSOPHY OF HISTORY

AMONG the characteristics of the present age, which is marked by many revolts against the rationalistic and mechanistic intellectual tendencies of the last century, is the revival of a more organic concept of the historical process and a renewal of philosophical speculation upon the meaning — if there be any discoverable meaning — that is contained in or denoted by that process. There is a narrowing of the old positivist breach between history and philosophy. The philosophers are becoming more historical, and, what is even more evident, the historians are becoming more philosophical; and the fact has been manifest now since the turn of the present century.

The reason for this revived probing of history for revelation of its inner mysteries is undoubtedly the preoccupation of the mind with the grave crisis through which our world has been passing since the latter years of the nineteenth century. The inadequacy of the old unphilosophical history, which reflected an order of deceptive peace and social stability, was bound to be felt in the tempestuous period that was ushered in by imperialism, socialism, and pessimism, and carried through the great war, the Communist

Revolution, and the last great debâcle of capitalism, to the present critical days, when all thoughtful persons are wondering how our civilization is to escape disaster. Without doubt we find ourselves today in one of those catastrophic periods which, ever since our civilization acquired a historical consciousness, have seen the mind turn to the philosophy of history.

The breakup of the Roman Empire, which provoked St. Augustine to write his *Civitas Dei* — the first great effort to set forth the philosophy of universal history — was such a period. So was the age extending from the Enlightenment to the French Revolution and romantic reaction; during which time innumerable philosophies of history were composed, notably those of Condorcet, Herder, Schlegel, de Maistre, Bonald, Hegel, Saint-Simon, and Comte. And the present age has seen the spread of Marxian historical analysis, the work of Spengler and the wide sweep of his influence, the Italian historical idealism of Croce and Gentile, and the deeply Christian and metaphysical speculations on history of the Russian philosopher, Nicholas Berdyaev, whose volume entitled *The Meaning of History* has occasioned this essay.

It is in fact an integral part of Berdyaev's thesis that only an age such as ours is able to grasp the 'historical,' to pierce through, as it were, to the metaphysical reality which, profoundly mysterious, is signified by the tragic destiny of man in the order of nature and time. He sets forth — and quite rightly, I believe — that there are three periods or stages in man's relation to and knowledge of the 'historical.' The first is a period of integral and organic experience in some settled historical order, fully matured and crystallized, as for example medieval Christendom. "This type of organic epoch does not favor either historical awareness or the elaboration of a philosophy of history. . . . Here thought is static; and . . . the dynamism of the object of historical science is not yet clearly grasped by the human mind."[1] Next comes a period of "fateful and menacing disruption" of that organic order. Its destiny is fulfilled and it breaks apart. In this age man is uprooted and alienated from tradition; he loses consciousness of the 'historical,' no longer feeling himself "directly and wholly a part of the historical object." This is an era of 'enlightenment,' such as the modern seventeenth and eighteenth centuries, and during it historical science and criticism are born; but there is on the other hand a loss of communion with the 'historical,' that is, a loss of knowledge of the past from within, a dulling of that memory which is tradition. Thirdly, there is the period that implies a return to the 'historical,' when "the human spirit, having experienced the collapse of a given historical order and the moment of schism and disintegration, is able to appose and oppose these two moments — that of direct participation in a historical order and that of the divorce from it — in order to arrive at a third state which induces . . . a particular aptitude for speculation and a corresponding aspiration towards the mysteries of the 'historical.' Such a state is especially favorable to the consideration of the problems of the philosophy of history."[2] This third stage of consciousness appeared in the romantic and idealist reaction against the antihistorical rationalism of Cartesian thought, and was manifested in the historical speculations of such men as Herder, Friedrich Schlegel, and Hegel. It continues and deepens today, the more so from the fact that, since the

---

[1] *The Meaning of History*, pp. 2, 3. Charles Scribner's Sons, publishers.
[2] *Ibid.*, pp. 4, 5.

romantic age of a century ago, Marxian historical material-ism has carried the revolt against the 'historical' to the uttermost limits, accomplishing at last "the de-animation of history and the annihilation of its inner mysteries."

Berdyaev's thought thus stands in relation to Marxism very much as that of, say, Friedrich Schlegel stands in relation to the atheistic and rationalist progressivism of the Enlightenment and French Revolution. His position is that of idealist and mystical reaction against a materialistic nominalism and nonrecognition of mystery. For some years now his books have been appearing in English translation, and they have met with much acclaim and respect. Profound reflections on the Russian Revolution, Marxian philosophy, and the bourgeois mind have come from him; and the volume entitled *The End of Our Time* revealed him as a major prophet of our day. All this work is permeated by a philosophy of history that is now set forth explicitly in a separate study.

Being Christian, Berdyaev's philosophy of history has in-evitable affinity to St. Augustine's grand historical drama of the City of God at war throughout time with the City of Satan. History originates in celestial cataclysm; its dialectic is the unceasing opposition of good and evil; its nature is that of the tragic destiny of the generations of men; its culmination will be in the reintegration of the terrestrial with the celestial order. History is therefore that tragic destiny which humankind follows through time from the Fall of Man to the consummation of the world, when there will be "no more barriers between our world beyond, as there were none in the depths of the past, before the dawn of life. . . . Our world aeon is coming to an end, the membrane separating it from other worlds will burst like that of a ripe fruit. This is the symbolical interpretation of the Apocalypse. The bond of time is broken, the closed cycle of terrestrial reality is invaded by the energies of a higher plane, the history of our world in time arrives together at its climax and its meaning. . . . History is not an endless development in time, nor is it subject to natural law, precisely because it is destiny (that is, determined to its end by the nature of its celestial origin). This is the ultimate finding of the metaphysics of history."[3]

Now, to the mind alienated from the Christian religious tradition this concept of the meaning of history can only appear, of course, as the fruit of a very mystical imagination. But it must be understood that such a mind is not competent to criticize the concept, but only to reject it completely. He who denies the piercing of the natural order by transcendent energies, and therefore denies also that there has been any revelation to man of transcendent truth, must, if he be logical, reject the very concept of the philosophy of history. For the human intelligence is imprisoned in the order of nature and historic time, and from its very constitution cannot comprehend the process of which it is itself the subject — unless, of course, it be given supernatural illumination. That is why there neither was nor could be anything properly called the philosophy of history before the Judaic and Christian revelation. As I have sought to show in the first of these essays, the pagan and oriental conception of the world process was one of repetitive cycles without beginning, end, or meaning; for to the pagan and oriental mind the metaphysical could not manifest itself in the historical. No conception of history as having linear form and directive meaning could enter the human mind unless there were to occur a unique series

---

[3] *Op. cit.*, pp. 205, 206.

of events pointing to a historical culmination; that is to say, prophecy and revelation were prerequisite to the conception of the philosophy of history. For the philosophy of history is necessarily prophetic and eschatological; it announces the meaning signified in the origin and destiny of the historical process. Hence modern philosophies of history such as those of Condorcet, Saint-Simon, and Marx — which posit the eschatological culmination of history in the perfection of the social order and a utopian kingdom of man over the mechanics of nature — are not really independent and rival philosophies; rather are they secularist degradations of the Judaic-Christian eschatology, but for which they could not have occurred to the western mind. For the pagan mind, let it be repeated, cannot conceive a linear historical progress toward a culminating historical end, nor discover any metaphysical reality in the cyclical repetition of human life-experience. And moreover, as we have also seen in another of these essays, but for the consciousness of freedom and the exaltation of man as king over nature, there could not have been any progress for modern historical philosophers to contemplate; man had to know himself as free, and the demons had to go out from nature before it could be boldly faced and subjected to mastery by man. Our civilization was moving fatally toward death and men were cringing before nature, when the religion of freedom and the kingdom of man entered it and made possible its miraculous recovery. As Berdyaev says with perfect truth, it was the Christian revelation — that union of the metaphysical and historical, and of the divine with the natural, in the Incarnation and Redemption — which broke the closed cycle of terrestrial life, and "introduced the notion of dynamism and the liberating principle which released that tempestuous and rebellious history of the western peoples, which has become pre-eminently history."

Such are the reasons why one may rightly say that if the Judaic-Christian revelation is not truth but only human fancy, there can be no philosophy of history. For that philosophy is essentially religious; it is a deduction from theology and revelation, not truth discoverable in the empirical order. There are not indeed several philosophies of history as there are several religions and metaphysical systems; there is but one philosophy of history, as there is but one religion that implants historical consciousness in the mind of man. That philosophy is Christian, and all other so-called 'philosophies of history' are but degraded and untenable derivatives from it.

That is not to say, however, that any one elaboration of this philosophy constitutes its true and correct statement. There is no orthodox version. The Church has never presumed to know the rationale of the historical process, but only to know certain transcendental truths which can indeed throw light upon the meaning of the historical process but do not constitute the philosophy of history. This field of speculation, logically closed to all who reject transcendency, is therefore an area of legitimate conflict between Christian thinkers. Berdyaev has entered it with a treatise of great importance, which cannot but provoke our admiration at the same time that it invites strong controversial attack.

The first and chief objection which I believe may properly be made against it touches its profoundly mystical character. Every philosopher contemplating the 'historical' will, of course, find himself facing the very deepest mystery, which the human mind, even with the aid of Christian knowledge, cannot plumb; yet Berdyaev tries to plumb it.

He probes for the origin of the 'historical' in the celestial order, "in the depths of the Absolute, in the divine life itself"; but instead of halting before this frontier of mystery, and realizing as Maritain has realized that beyond it only angelic and not human intelligence can know with understanding, Berdyaev invades this realm for a theological adventure in pursuit of an answer to the question of how mobility could have arisen in the Absolute. Page after page he writes concerning this humanly insoluble problem, opposing himself to rational theology, wading deep into the wilderness of German mysticism, and giving utterance to thoughts such as this: "In the dark nature of God, deeper than Him, lies a sort of primal dark abyss, and in its inmost depths occurs a theogonic process or that of divine genesis. This process is secondary when compared with that primal 'groundlessness' and inexpressible abyss which is irrational and incommensurable with any of our categories. There is a primal source and fount of being from which an eternal torrent pours out and in which the divine light shines everlastingly, while the act of divine genesis is taking place. The acceptance of such a dark and irrational premises is one of the means toward the discovery and apprehension of the possible existence of movement in the inmost depths of the divine life. . . . Every glib rationalistic theory of the Divine denies this. All superficial doctrines, fearing to extend tragic movement to the divine life because they envisage the latter without inner contradiction or conflict, that is, reduced to an extreme form of logical and rational conception, also deny this. But it constitutes the great discovery of German metaphysics. . . . It determined to a large extent the future of German philosophy, whose fundamental discovery it indeed represents. It states that the primal foundations of being rest upon a certain irrational and willful principle, and that the whole significance and essence of the world process consist in the illumination of this dark irrational principle in cosmogony and theogony."[4] Now, this is what Berdyaev sets forth as the hypothesis of his metaphysics of history, and it is a leap of the mind into the region of the unknowable — a dangerous leap. It is the sort of theological mysticism that has issued again and again into irrational and heretical deviations from a sane Christian orthodoxy, which recognizes that the frontier of mystery is the borderland of human comprehension.

Moreover, it may even be that there is in this not only a certain intellectual presumptuousness but also a kind of impiety, and that it is not good for man in his present state to seek to look too closely upon the face of God, lest what he sees there send him to despair. Certainly it is evident that there is a near connection between Berdyaev's mystical probing and the deep pessimism which also permeates his historical speculation. This is the second point on which I believe he is open to attack.

His whole treatise is saturated with a pessimism concerning man in the terrestrial order. History reveals to him not a progress of man in this world, but a continuous succession of failures. Tragic defeat is the lot of every human generation. "Man's historical experience has been one of steady failure and there are no grounds for supposing that it will ever be anything else. Not one single project elaborated within the historical process has ever proved successful. None of the problems of any given historical epoch whatsoever has been solved, no aims attained, no hopes realized. . . . Examining specific periods of history and their respective problems, we feel them to be consumed with an inner

---

[4] *Op. cit.,* pp. 55, 56.

disease and impotent to arrive at a solution. To consider
only modern history, its profound failure is amazing."[5]
Indeed, this Russian philosopher, who has elsewhere pro-
nounced the doom of modern civilization, in this volume
passes sentence of doom on all human effort to solve great
terrestrial problems. One can detect here, I believe, that
old oriental pessimism which conceives man's nature as
wholly vitiated and not merely wounded by the Fall. And
one can detect also what appears as a deep inconsistency
between this pessimism and the more completely orthodox
elements in Berdyaev's philosophy of history. I mean that
this perpetual failure, from which only God rescues the
failing, is not consistent with his doctrine that the
Redemption is also a historical action, the very essence of
the 'historical': the union of the metaphysical and the
historical. But for the God who breaks his bonds, man is
broken on a wheel that turns forever. So does Berdyaev
conceive human destiny, and so I think he turns back to
that prerevelation cyclic conception of the world process,
instead of developing the implications of the irruption of
the Son of God into the historical world of fallen men.
I do not mean to suggest that history is not replete with
the sorriest failures, nor that the destiny of each generation of men is not tragic. It is most certainly the lot of
man to fail and to fail tragically; but his history is not all
failure. There is another aspect of the record in the history
of the redemptive action upon human society, in the
rewards won for us by the saints, in the ripening of the
fruits of the Faith. There is, in this sense, a historically
progressive Redemption which can be seen and measured
if one looks at it in the right perspective of time.

Now this exaggerated mysticism and historical pessi-

---

[5] *Op. cit.,* p. 198.

mism are related — and causally related, I believe — to yet a third grave weakness of Berdyaev's thought. He apparently accepts as valid the Spenglerian concept of cultures as spiritual organisms which come into being, mature, and die in obedience to the laws of organic destiny. He accepts also Spengler's thesis that 'civilization' is the doom of every culture, and indeed he prizes this as the main Russian contribution to philosophy. "Every culture at a certain stage of its development," he tells us, "discloses . . . a tendency to disintegrate in its religious and spiritual foundations. . . . This is achieved through the process of 'enlightenment' which is common to both ancient and later Occidental culture. And this fact reveals the fatal dialectic inherent in culture. . . . It exhausts itself spiritually and wastes its energies. It passes from the 'organic' to the 'critical' stage of its existence."[6] This latter stage is 'civilization,' it is the stage in which western culture is now well advanced, and therefore the end is in sight.

But is this true? Are cultures organisms? And if we say they are, how much light does that throw upon them? To call them organisms is surely rather to employ a figure of speech than a scientifically descriptive term, but admitting at least that they display — as all that is human cannot but display — an organic nature, we cannot truly say that the laws governing their destinies have been revealed. And surely God's choice of the classical culture of Hellenistic-Roman antiquity for the garment, as it were, of His mystical body liberated that culture from the fatal cycle of destiny. Did that culture really die, and was our culture (now said to be disintegrating) born, as Spengler has said, in western Europe about the year 900? The answer is no, for our culture is that of Christianized classicism and it is

---

[6] *Op. cit.*, p. 213.

still very much alive. There are excrescences upon and around it; there are alien infusions within it; there are detached and decaying parts of it lying about. But it has its continuous life; it has its unbroken institutions and the religion which is its soul; it has its memory that goes back to its origins. Many times has it appeared to be approaching death, but it has always recovered, purging and renewing its life not from without but from within. The atheistic elements of modern civilization do not signify the death of our culture but only new problems for it to solve. Whatever may be the fate of other cultures, we should know by this time that our culture does not die. Belloc's famous thesis in his *Europe and the Faith* is a far better interpretation of our history than this Spengler-Berdyaev thesis of decay and destiny.

Such are the chief complaints which I believe may be justly lodged against this study in the philosophy of history although in bringing them forward I do not mean to suggest that Berdyaev has not written a very great book. It is in other respects a masterpiece of modern thought, one of the mature fruits of the European mind.

6

EUROPE AND CHRISTENDOM

A SERIES of essays treating of the cultural conflict raging in our times recently appeared from the pen of that engaging writer, Mr. Joseph Wood Krutch. They were published under the title, *Was Europe a Success?,* and they contained rather more thoughtful substance than might be suggested by so odd a caption. The author of *The Modern Temper* is an unhappy, disheartened, and pessimistic liberal who can see little ahead for men like himself, save perhaps fighting a rear-guard action against gathering forces of destruction. The substance of these essays is not unfamiliar, but a special interest attaches to them because Mr. Krutch has been a foremost prophet of despair and because he can discern more clearly than most liberals the ultimate implications of contemporary revolutionary movements.

He has been gravely impressed by the fact that "nothing is more characteristic of much contemporary thought than its tendency to be literally 'radical,' that is, to carry its criticism on to a point where it becomes, not a criticism of certain defects or maladjustments of society, but by implication at least a criticism of the whole complex of institutions, traditions, and standards of value . . . within the meaning of the term 'Europe' — and which is, indeed, almost exactly

what is now more often referred to as 'bourgeois civilization.' "[1] It is Mr. Krutch's quite correct realization of this
fact that provoked him to write these essays. He recognizes
what so many other liberals fail to see; namely, that the
success of Communism "depends not only on a new form of
government but also on the destruction of 'European' culture and the creation of a new man"; which new man, "if
he ever actually came into existence, would be really new,
taxonomically a mere variety of *homo sapiens,* but no more
than the ancient Mayan identical with the man of European
philosophy or poetry." Therefore, says Mr. Krutch, "the
issue is both clearer and more fundamental than that which
is commonly drawn between the various schools of political
opinion. . . . Behind the impatience of the champions of a
new beginning and behind the caution of those liberals who
hesitate to abandon too quickly or too completely certain
accustomed ways, lies the unwillingness of the one to cut
loose from the European soul as well as the European political system, and the fear of the other that certain achievements of that soul — unique in the general history of mankind — will not easily be duplicated."[2] A whole culture is at
stake: "something which includes not merely a way of life
and a heritage of philosophy and art but the very sensibil-
ities and forms of thought which made that heritage possible. . . . By the revolutionists themselves we are forbidden
to suppose that only our material possessions — if we
happen to have any — are threatened, or that — if we have
none — there is 'nothing to lose but our chains.' Something
else is threatened and that something we may agree to designate by the convenient word 'Europe.' "

Few thoughtful persons would wish to deny that, in

---

[1] *Was Europe a Success?*, p. 11. Farrar and Rinehart publishers.
[2] *Op. cit.*, pp. 12, 13.

making these observations, Mr. Krutch is substantially right.
Nor would there be many to dispute his statement that "the
man which Europe produced realized more of his potentialities than did the man developed in any other portion of the
globe." We can certainly agree with Mr. Krutch that "the
European man has been the most successful in exploring
that realm of consciousness which appears to be exclusively
human."[3] There are a number of statements in these essays
that strike the mind as true and even penetrating, as for
example that 'Europe' today is "threatened quite as defi-
nitely by liberals and reformers as it is by radicals — the
only difference between the two being that the one is slowly
undermining the foundations without knowing what he is
about while the other is deliberately blowing them up." I
might select other passages also to illustrate this power of
Mr. Krutch's mind to probe below the surface of things, but
the distressing fact would remain that the essays as a whole
actually do not show Mr. Krutch probing very deep.

The first reason for saying this is that he has left us in
perplexity as to what 'Europe' and 'European man' are. At
one point he makes mention of that "European spirit which
was born in Athens, rationalized in Rome, and taken over
by the Catholic Church"; which would seem to imply that
'Europe' and 'European man' were formed by the classical
heritage and the Christian faith, as in truth they were. But
at other points Mr. Krutch writes of the Catholic Middle
Ages almost as if his European man were then nonexistent.
This man, he tells us, first appeared in Greek antiquity and
then was almost destroyed when the civilization of the
ancient world went down; "it required," according to Mr.
Krutch, "between 1000 and 1500 years for him to begin the
re-establishment of himself."[4] The implication here is that

[3] *Op. cit.*, p. 15.
[4] *Op. cit.*, p. 21.

'European man' is not at all the product of the Middle Ages, but is identical with a certain kind of man in antiquity who re-emerged in modern times by sloughing off something that must necessarily have been non-'European.' Yet in describing some of his characteristics Mr. Krutch stresses certain marks which betray the Christian formation of this man. "One of them is a sense of the reality, the worth, and the sacredness of the individual, who is thought of as having in himself a value for which there is no equivalent." This was not a characteristic of the ancient Greek; its origin lies in Christian doctrine; whether he knows it or not, the modern European man who has this sense has simply saved an old coin out of the Christian treasury. And very much the same may be said of another characteristic which Mr. Krutch attributes to his 'European man': "a similar sense of the importance of something which has been variously defined but always called 'freedom' for this same individual."[5] For the European who knows and prizes this freedom does so because the Catholic Church fought all the fatalists of history in behalf of the doctrine of free will; this too is part of the Christian capital upon which the modern world is still living. But Mr. Krutch's 'European man' has also some essential characteristics which are by no means Christian. For instance, he "regards progress and achievement as a movement away from the usual, the norm, the universally acceptable," and he is attached to the "intellectual luxury" of a nonpartisan, spectator-like detachment from the turmoil of social conflict. These are plainly the marks of the uprooted modern bourgeois intellectual, torn loose from the old religious and corporate life of Christendom: a man who has been very conspicuous upon the European scene since the close of the Middle Ages. Mr.

[5] *Ibid.*

Krutch's 'European man' thus appears to be essentially the modern liberal who nourishes some surviving Christian prejudices, and who has enjoyed until recently a comfortable life in a civilization which he now finds himself unable to defend.

I do not believe that Mr. Krutch could fairly accuse me of having disfigured or caricatured his European man in what I have just said. It would, however, be rather easy to take some of his statements and from their import construct a definition of his European man that would be very absurd. It would include the ancient Greeks, but exclude the modern Catholics; it would leave out St. Thomas Aquinas and Dante, but include Spinoza, Freud, and Einstein; it would exclude the peasants of Spain and the Pope of Rome, but it would include Mr. Joseph Wood Krutch; indeed it would claim Europe for the pagans, the Jews, and the heretics, and expatriate all the orthodox Catholics. Certainly Mr. Krutch thinks of his man as being most 'European' before he was Christianized and after he became partly or wholly de-Christianized; as a Christian Mr. Krutch does not seem to like him very well or to regard him as quite 'European.'

Mr. Krutch is far too generous, of course, to make these exclusions, but it must be said that he is so only because he has not got a clear idea as to precisely what he means when he speaks of 'Europe.' Indeed he does not appear to mean anything more definite than that Europe, considered as a culture, is something he is fond of, something that is congenial to his spirit. He likes its humanist tradition, its rich variety of material and intellectual culture, and he doubts if a radically different kind of man could match these creative achievements. In the tangled story of Europe Mr. Krutch has a fascinated interest, but he has not untangled

that story and rendered it intelligible. If he had, he would
not discern European man in the ancient Greek; nor would
he equate European civilization with Greek civilization. It
is perfectly true that European civilization is the outcome of
an organic growth continuous from antiquity, but it is not
true that Greece was Europe; nor was the ancient Greek a
European; he only helped to make the European. The cultural community that is Europe came into existence as the
society of Christendom during the Middle Ages, and because this society had a new conception of the nature and
destiny of man it formed a new and very different man
from the man of antiquity. It was this new man who made
Europe, who gave it its distinctive character, and who alone,
therefore, is entitled to be called the characteristic European.
Periclean Athens was not Europe, nor was the pagan Roman
Empire; but Christendom was Europe and it has never
abandoned the rather disconcerting habit of reminding us
occasionally that it still is Europe. This is the great fact
that Mr. Krutch has evidently never probed deep enough to
discover, although he may have had some fleeting glimpses
of it; and it is his confusion on this point that explains the
weakness of all his essays. The radicals whom he fears are
clearer and more fundamental in their thinking than he is;
they could tell him what Europe really is. They prove their
knowledge when they aim their heaviest blows at its foundation source of strength; it is because they know that
Europe is Christendom that they are so fiercely at war with
its religion. They know that once that is extinguished the
rest of the work (demolishing Mr. Krutch's denatured and
anemic Europe) will be a quick and easy job.

Had Mr. Krutch a clearer understanding of the essential
substance of Europe, I do not think he would take it so
lightly for granted that the last war was a great European

failure. "No failure," he says, "could be more utter than the
failure which culminated in the World War, and it may
seem hard to believe that any one could insist without irony
upon the necessity of saving that civilization."[6] But this
statement makes sense only on the assumption that the War
was a suicidal convulsion of European civilization (doubtless it was exactly that for what Mr. Krutch believes to be
'Europe'); but it is quite possible that the War actually was
a demonstration of the vitality of the authentic Europe.
There issued from it, for example, the overthrow of the
Muscovite Empire and its old ally, anti-European Prussia;
there came the resurrection of Catholic Poland and
Bohemia; one thinks also of Ireland. The empire of the
Moslem Turks was destroyed and the Christian nationalities
of eastern Europe came to new life. Italy experienced a
veritable return of the Romans, and the ascendancy of
Europe came back (for a time at least) to its ancestral home
in the Roman lands of the south; Rome recovered her old
pivot position in Europe; the way was paved for the liberation of the Pope, and the Catholic revival gained fresh
strength. What really happened in the world, as Chesterton
remarked a few years ago, was "the reawakening of old
places and the return to old shrines." I would not insist
upon this as an adequate interpretation of the World War,
but it may be said that it is the only intelligible fundamental
meaning that anyone has ever read into that conflict. And
if it was the true meaning, then the War was not a European
failure but a rather considerable success.

Again it is Mr. Krutch's failure to probe through to the
true Europe which accounts for his unfortunate error in
finding evil fruit growing upon good trees and good fruit
borne by evil trees. As an example of this, he says: "Not

---

[6] *Op. cit.,* p. 16.

only did chivalry bring slaughter, and religion persecution, but the very cultivation of intellect and beauty always implied their cultivation at the expense of thousands shut out from the enjoyment of the arts or even the comfort of adequate goods."[7] Now, everything in that statement is wrong. Chivalry did not bring slaughter. The barbarized world of the early Middle Ages was certainly full of slaughter, but this was actually abated as the chivalric ethic came to the fore. Chivalry arose as the Church gradually attained some success in transfiguring the mere warrior into a defender of society and directing his energies toward noble ends. He was enlisted under the patronage of the Queen of the Saints and taught a more righteous and discriminating use of the sword. Chivalry indeed was a great effort to crush the slaughter of barbaric social conflict, and it bequeathed to Europe its finest moral tradition. It is equally a distortion of the truth to say that religion brought persecution, unless Mr. Krutch means (as he obviously does not) the persecution of religion by an opposing and hostile world. The Church fought its enemies, to be sure, and with weapons suitable to the successive ages through which it has lived; but it did not introduce religious persecution into the world, and the influence of its ethic was always in the direction of leading men toward a life of peace and brotherhood. There have always been men who commit grievous abuses in defense of religion, but its noblest exemplars have never been persecutors. Nor is it true to say that the cultivation of intellect and beauty have always implied the deprivation of the good things of life from the mass of men. How could one reconcile Thomas Aquinas in his mendicant friar's habit with this statement? In modern times, yes, the cultivation (one might better say the enjoyment) of these things

---

[7] *Op. cit.*, pp. 15, 16.

has been extensively carried on by a class living without
justice on the fruits of other men's labor; but it was not so
in the popular and corporate life of old Christendom. The
highest intellectual cultivation in those times was reached
by men sworn to poverty and committed to the cause of the
poor. And this still goes on, even though it may elude the
notice of metropolitan intellectuals.

Taking another example of the same thing, Mr. Krutch
says that Europe must rid itself of imperialism, military
pride, and the national spirit, if it is "to continue at all,"
although without these, he admits, we could not have had
"the glory that was Greece, the grandeur that was Rome, or
the right little, tight little island which is still called
England." These are things, says Mr. Krutch, that "we
hate," and yet without them we could not have had Shakes-
peare or Racine. "This thing called civilization," he writes,
"grew up under certain conditions and flourished as a result
of them. It was associated with the very tendencies which
progressives as well as radicals deplore."[8] But Mr. Krutch
thinks very loosely when by implication he equates imperialism, military pride, and the national spirit with mere
armed conquest, soldierly arrogance, and chauvinistic nationalism; he confuses an abuse or exaggeration of a thing
with the thing itself, saying that we must be rid of it; and
then he goes on to say that nevertheless these evils produced
great goods which it would be very hard to see go also. But
is there not a righteous imperialism, something more than
naked conquest and subjugation, an imperialism of justice,
law, and missionary civilization? Is there not a military
pride consisting in the observance of a manly and heroic
code of duty, honor, and loyalty, of defense of the community and justice, to be distinguished from hard and boast-

---

[8] *Op. cit.*, pp. 17, 18.

ful swashbuckling? Is there not a national spirit that consists in a dear love of one's land and people, to be sharply marked off from an arrogant and aggressive nationalism? And if these things exist without their abuses and exaggerations, do we 'hate them'? Do we really want to get along without them? Could we indeed get along without them? I do not think so, and I do not believe that Mr. Krutch thinks so, for he would find, if he looked closely enough, that it has only been when and insofar as these things have been clean of their abuses that they have produced fruits to enrich European life.

It would be possible to go on very much further striking down point after point in these essays, and in every case the error would be seen to lie rooted in a misreading of the true nature of Europe. For Europe may be likened unto a garden where many beautiful flowers have grown, and although Mr. Krutch has seen and admired many of these flowers he has not traced their stems and roots down through the now tangled underbrush of weeds. The flowers are fading because the weeds are choking off their life, and some men say that we must pull them up and transplant them in another soil where they may find a different nourishment. Mr. Krutch suspects they will not grow in another soil, and he is right. But he does not know why he is right.

7

THE JACOBIN HERESY

INTENSIVE study of the great Revolution by which France and, in good time, much of the western world was made anew, has been unceasingly in progress since the establishment of the present French Republic, and especially since Taine, in the early and disheartening days of the Republic, published his *Origines de la France contemporaine.* The sources have been dug to light, catalogued, and criticized; from studying the dramatic Parisian events scholars have turned to ascertaining what the Revolution did in the provinces and beyond the frontiers of France; economic and sociological history has supplemented the political account; religious and psychological factors also have been explored, at least in part. Monograph studies have piled high while new syntheses continue to be written, and although the specialist doubtless will say, as always, that much work remains to be done, it seems unlikely that future research can bring to light anything to alter the main lines of the picture that now may be seen. Yet divergent interpretations are still maintained, and there is still no agreement among historians as to what was the essential nature of that which Hilaire Belloc once called "the Revolutionary Thing."

Those words doubtless connote to many minds nothing but a mystical abstraction. For how can the Revolution be thought of as a 'thing'? It was nothing concrete and tangible, but a process of spectacular change, a succession of events adding up to make one great event which left the human society wherein it happened a very changed society. Some force was at work, striving amid a set of opposing or favoring circumstances, now winning its way, now meeting successful resistance; and that force was the will of men to change the order of their affairs. There was an ideal vision before their eyes, a creed upon their lips, a doctrine in their minds; and that is what is meant by 'the Revolutionary Thing.' It was man willing to act in pursuit of a vision and in allegiance to a creed; this it was that sought to make a new France, and were it not so the old France could not but have gone on down its rotting way to ruin. Of course the whole story of the revolutionary era is not the story of that thing, for other and different forces also were at work. There was corruption, there was cruelty, there was selfish ambition, madness, misunderstanding, and fear; these also guided the will of men and helped to make that complex of events called the French Revolution. But men who acted from such common human motives did not make 'the Revolutionary Thing.' Men so moved are present at all times, and in any revolution they will affect importantly the course of events; they will aid the cause for base and selfish ends, or they will oppose it, or betray it; they will constrict its action or give it bad direction; but they will not make it, will not be one with that which seeks to right the world.

Now it is the high merit of the work of Professor Crane Brinton, of Harvard, that it helps make clear a right concept of 'the Revolutionary Thing.' His volume entitled *A Decade of Revolution,* which bears the same marks of high excellence that characterized his earlier study of the Jacobins, comes near to being a really brilliant book, and it affords the occasion for this essay.

Professor Brinton displays in this work an intelligence that is really piercing, and his judgments are admirably independent. Nor is he content merely to relate events, but seeks also to explain and define; and if he is not always successful in this effort he is not the less instructive for failing. Certainly he is to be commended warmly for breaking boldly with that 'official' school of historians founded by the late Alphonse Aulard and now divided in allegiance between Aulard and his rebellious disciple, the late Albert Mathiez; which split, as Brinton points out, "follows the division in French party politics between the *radicaux socialistes* and the socialists and communists." The founder of this school was a typical man of the bourgeois Third Republic, a patriotic nationalist but narrow in his sympathies and strongly anti-Catholic. He was not in any sense a great historian, but like G. G. Coulton or H. C. Lea, one of those second-rate historians who have been very able scholars, critical of their sources, careful and accurate in their documentation. Aulard came of age as historical study was becoming 'scientific' with its own special technique for the critical use of sources, and his work was based strictly upon contemporary records; hence his distrust of memoirs and dislike of interpretative generalization; hence the enormous authority still attaching to his name among the older American scholars of today. Aulard, of course, no more than any other man, could put historical data into intelligible order without venturing to select, generalize, interpret, and explain; but whenever he did so he was weak. Witness, for example, his attempt to explain the Terror as a mere government of national defense caused by the pressure of foreign and domestic war. It was this combination in Aulard of reluctance to explain with feebleness in trying to explain that led to Mathiez's revolt, although the latter was also a professional historian of rigorous scholarly training. The younger man took a proletarian rather than bourgeois viewpoint, and gave a class-struggle version of the Terror. That brought the split, although superficially the difference between master and student was their opposing judgments on Danton and Robespierre.

Now, in saying that Brintan breaks with Aulard and Mathiez I do not mean that he does not respect their solid learning, nor that he abstains from drawing heavily upon their findings. I mean rather than he does not accept their explanations, and the main point of departure is the explanation of the Jacobin Terror. The search for that Professor Brinton carries far beyond Aulard, and does not rest with Mathiez's Marxian explanation, although he recognizes this as part of a much larger explanation. "The men who made the Terror," he writes, "were not thinking in terms of economics, were not even, incredible though it may seem, lusting in terms of economics." There was indeed a great deal more in the picture of the Terror than Marxist eyes can see. "Thanks to the work of Aulard and his followers (it) contains an emphatic, indeed, overwhelming background of foreign and civil war; thanks to Mathiez, it has been completed with a touch of the class struggle. To drop the metaphor: into the historical situation known as the Terror there went the desperate necessities of men who wage war in some measure not of their choice; there went the hatred of the poor for the rich, of the failure for the success; there went the relatively simple and eternal desire of men to rule other men; there went the desire of the overeducated and inexperienced men to realize the paper utopias of eighteenth-century thought; and there went the religious fanaticism of men born in a frenzy of hope beyond the petty decencies of common sense. But omit a single one of these elements and you no longer have the Terror. Modern historiography, with its pseudoscientific bias, has emphasized the material circumstances, the economic motive, anything but the deliberate volition of men whose interests, ambitions, and ideas were in themselves varied and unpredictable compounds."[1]

There you have it: 'the volition of men,' and of men who were not even 'lusting in terms of economics!' But what was the great thing they wanted? What stirred in them that frenzied will, that fierce intolerance which leads men who are by no means evil to kill? I have called it a creed and a vision, and Professor Brinton names it well "the religion of Jacobinism," which was an apocalyptic faith in the possibility, nay, the certainty, of a complete transformation of human society, a swift escape from corruption and pain to perfection and felicity. Man was to attain full realization for his perfectible nature through destruction of old tyrannies and superstitions; an age was to be opened when, in Condorcet's words, "the human race, free from all its fetters, withdrawn from the empire of chance as from that of the enemies of Progress, would walk with firm and assured step in the way of truth, of virtue and of happiness." A generation of men had lost faith in the God of Christian orthodoxy, but they affirmed a new faith: the faith of Rousseau's Savoyard vicar: faith in man raised to grace anew by baptism in the waters of a deified Nature. It is ever the mark of a new religion that the devout are determined to create a new kind of man, and that was the avowed aim of the Jacobin believers. "You must entirely refashion a people

---

[1] Brinton, *A Decade of Revolution*, p. 162. Harper and Brothers, publishers.

whom you wish to make free," proclaimed the Committee of Public Safety, "destroy its prejudices, alter its habits, limit its necessities, root up its vices, purify its desires." Jacobinism was the religious creed of men militantly bent on reaching the 'heavenly city of the eighteenth-century philosophers,' and it is the major merit of Professor Brinton's work that it recognizes this fact. "The devotional language of the Jacobins," he writes, "their frequent accesses of collective emotion, their conviction of righteousness, their assurance that their opponents are sinners, direct agents of the devil, their intolerance, their desire for martyrdom, their total want of humour — all these are unmistakable signs of the theological temperament. It is possible to build up from the scattered records of what these Jacobins said and did a fairly systematic scheme of values cast into a form closely parallel to traditional Christianity. Mankind is divided into the saved and the damned. Salvation is achieved by grace. Grace is the free gift of a benign God. . . . The saved are at eternal war with the damned. The regeneration of the race is ultimately possible, but can be achieved only by the conversion of the damned, or what is much more in accord with Calvinistic and Robespierrean theology, by their extermination."[2]

Now these are the words of a very discerning historian, and one finds it a little puzzling that the man who wrote them did not see a little further than apparently he has seen. I mean that the man who can see that Jacobinism was a religion ought also to see that the thing can be even better named by calling it a Christian heresy. For whence came this new creed but from the old common traditions of Christendom? What could Liberty, Equality, Fraternity have meant to men had they not been heir to a tradition of free will, equality before God, and a corporate bond

---

[2] *Op. cit.,* p. 169.

of human fellowship? The old society had been very disloyal to that tradition and therefore men arose to accuse it; but their accusation was really an appeal to the very tradition that had been betrayed. These men revolted against a religion which they adjudged to be corrupt superstition, but they actually took their stand for values which it had been the glory of that religion to affirm. And that is the way it has ever been with the great Christian heresies. In an age of religious decline some men will seize upon the neglected values, affirm them anew, confront the priests with their condemnation, and by mistaking the right position of the neglected values in the whole scheme of values use them to fashion a heresy. That is what Luther did with faith in divine mercy, and what Calvin did with faith in divine omnipotent justice. It is also what the Jacobins did with Christian doctrines respecting freedom, social justice, and human rights. They abandoned the doctrine of the Fall and the Redemption through the merits of Christ, but with the residue of morality, now torn loose from its roots in the supernatural, they made a new creed with a new core of emphasis. Mr. Chesterton put it rightly when he said that "what really happened was this: that the men of the eighteenth century, many of them in a just impatience with corrupt and cynical priests, turned on those priests and said in effect, 'Well, I suppose you call yourselves Christians; so you can't actually *deny* that men are brothers or that it is our duty to help the poor.' The very confidence of their challenge, the very ringing note in the revolutionary voice, came from the fact that the Christian reactionaries were in a false position as Christians. The democratic demand won because it seemed unanswerable." Now, a new religion never seems unanswerable, and right here you have the reason why this thing was rather a heresy than a new religion, why it gained such a mighty success: it contained very precious and familiar truths. It is the mark of every heresy that it has some content of the old truth; which content is the secret of its driving force; and all the great heresies have been strong exactly in the measure that they have been orthodox; all have lived only on inherited capital; which is the reason why they never live to witness the revival of the old tradition whence they spring. The Jacobin heresy has been no exception to this rule, for as Professor Brinton remarks, "that strange force which gives life to mere words has today pretty well gone from Liberty, Equality, Fraternity." The mood has gone and the old revolutionary faith in man is dying away; that creed of confident hope now seems hollowly unreal, a memorial to another human failure. Yet the orthodoxy that affirmed the revolutionary truths, not as a mere mood, or sentiment, or hope, but as a doctrine — as an integral part of one larger body of doctrine — is not dead and is not stale; rather it seems today to be strangely and freshly alive.

If Professor Brinton had recognized the Jacobin creed as a Christian heresy I do not think he would have been puzzled, as he evidently has been, by the "paradox that, in spite of the melodramatic horror of events in France, the French Revolution has in the long run proved even more revolutionary in its effects on other countries than in its effects on France."[3] He makes the point (and quite correctly) that the nineteenth- and twentieth-century socialist movement is a derivation from Jacobinism. The one, he says, is the direct outgrowth of the other; and this being true, he is puzzled to account for the fact that "the French Revolution, itself in so many ways the product of the

Op. cit., p. 278.

modern spirit of unrest and experiment, helped to per-
petuate in France a relatively stationary and balanced rural
economy."[4] Why, in other words, have the people who
went so frantically Jacobin been able to resist what evolved
straight out of Jacobinism? The answer is that, the traditional life of her society being revived and strengthened
by salutary reform, France was able to excrete what was evil
or mad in the Revolution — enough so at least to maintain
a fair measure of national well-being. There has been little
real socialism in France (for all that there have been
many so-called socialists in her government) because the
driving force and genuine value in the triumphant Jacobin
revolution was the sane social morality of Christian men;
and wherever this is restored Socialism sounds its bird call
in vain. Socialism is certainly a continuation of Jacobinism
— a continuation in corruption and error; but the one does
not follow the other with the necessity of historical logic.
And what if Jacobinism seek absolution of its sins and
return to that from which it sprang and where alone it is
at home and at peace? That is essentially what happened
in France, considering the nation as a whole, and that is
the explanation of Brinton's paradox.

   I said above that it is puzzling that this writer should
discern the religious nature of Jacobinism and yet fail to
see it as a Christian heresy. But actually the answer is given.
There was a new religion because the old religion was dead,
killed at last by the Revolution. Here is the report of its
death: "The French Revolution did destroy, as completely
as it can be destroyed, the nexus of loyalties which had
once made the old regime an authority. It might be more
accurate to say that the French Revolution merely made
evident to all a work of destruction begun long before, but

---

[4] *Op. cit.*, p. 278.

the fact of that destruction was undeniable in 1799. French-
men had ceased to feel the authority . . . of the God of
St. Paul, St. Louis, and even Louis XIV. We have all of
us today been so much affected by this abandonment of
the Christian God . . . that only by a difficult leap of the
imagination can we live again even for a moment in the
old world of ideas. But in this old world men really did
believe . . . that life on this earth is a fleeting transition to
eternity, that such a life is inevitably one of misery, that,
however, there are rigid rules of conduct for such a life,
conformity with which will be rewarded with eternal
bliss, disobedience of which will be punished by eternal
damnation. Remnants of such ideas still exist among us,
but recognizably as remnants, not as part of a unified
whole."[5]

Now grasp the full import of this passage: the Catholic
religion was destroyed, and the God of the New Testament
(God of St. Paul, St. Louis, and Louis XIV) has gone from
men's minds; it is even hard to imagine what it was for
men to live in the old orthodoxy; only "remnants" of it
survive! Either this Harvard professor wrote thoughtlessly what he did not mean, or he is unaware of the
existence of a few hundred million orthodox Christians —
say roughly one fifth of the human race — or, if he is not
unaware of their existence, he presumes to deny that they
believe what they profess to believe. These millions daily
declare their credo in the whole Faith from the Trinity
to the resurrection of the body and the life everlasting, but
Professor Brinton says they do not mean it, and that insofar
as they believe any of this they cling to a few remnants.
So does a university professor wave away the existence of
the Christian Faith in an age of almost unparalleled

---

[5] *Op. cit.*, p. 281.

missionary activity, an age which is witnessing perhaps the greatest revival of orthodoxy since the Counter-Reformation.

These observations on the passing of the Faith may be marked as a prize example of a kind of intellectual myopia not infrequently encountered among even learned men who are cut loose from traditional religion. For them the thing is so dead that even when it marches before their eyes they can only see as one who looks without seeing. The thing is dead, and only a miracle could raise it, but they do not believe in miracles; what appears is not the thing itself, but the ghost of the thing, and they do not believe in ghosts. Hence they are driven to denying the evidence of the senses and affirming what is patently false.

8

CATHOLIC HISTORICAL SCHOLARSHIP AND
THE ANGLICAN SCHISM

I

SEVERAL years ago Hilaire Belloc wrote an essay entitled "The Counter Attack through History" in which he called for a vigorous repulse of the attack made upon the Church by those who write or make use of false history. "We have suffered," he said, "for over four hundred years an attack which was mainly an appeal to history; to repel that attack we must undertake the counter-offensive; and the moment is highly propitious for so salutary and inspiring an exercise."[1] This attack was begun at a time when, because of what Mr. Belloc called "an accretion of myth," the Church was most vulnerable to historical criticism; and, unfortunately, from the very beginning of the attack, the Catholic writers permitted themselves to be thrown upon the defensive. They expended altogether too much energy answering small points of objection, the while allowing much to go by default which ought to have been maintained; and they even were led to accept as true a great deal

---

[1] *Essays of a Catholic*, p. 126. By permission of the Macmillan Co., publishers.

of their enemies' false history. There came to be implanted in them "an ingrained habit of the defensive," which is "the prime condition of defeat." And as Mr. Belloc also insisted, "it was not the learning, still less the logic, of our enemies which gave them such strength in this field; it was the defensive mood into which Catholic apologists allowed themselves to be maneuvered."[2]

The lesson of this unhappy experience, Mr. Belloc concluded, is that the Catholic historians today should abandon the defensive and adopt a vigorous counteroffensive: "We have every reason for undertaking it . . . because the weight of historical argument is now on our side . . . the moment is particularly propitious because recent research, and the conclusions based on a wider knowledge of documents particularly support us today; while we have another practical reason for taking action, which is that the moment in which we are living is disillusioned. The belief of people in the historical fairy-tales of the last generation, as in all its older traditions both true and false, is shaken. . . . The younger generation today are perfectly willing to hear the truth — for instance, about the period of the Reformation. They are more than willing to revise the old-fashioned and already more than half-forgotten misrepresentation of Catholic times and nations, and meanwhile the instruments with which to act are ready to our hands."[3]

For the historical writer of today, addressing himself to readers and scholars who have been brought up intellectually on anti-Catholic history, there is certainly no more fruitful field in which to work than that of the history of the Church standing at bay in the world since the outbreak of the Protestant Revolution. The only real difficulty he

---

[2] *Op. cit.,* p. 131.
[3] *Ibid.,* pp. 139, 140.

faces, as Mr. Belloc pointed out, lies neither in the quality nor use of his materials, nor in the lack of adequate field for their exploitation, but in the problem of getting the right audience to hear what he has to say.

It is true that Mr. Belloc, who is the most spirited and without doubt the ablest leader of the historical counterattack, has not lacked an audience. He has a fairly large one (made up not only of Catholics but also of thousands of non-Catholics), for he is widely and rightly acclaimed as one of the greatest English writers in the modern age. His excellent historical studies, therefore, have made a broad and deep impression on the more thoughtful sections of the general reading public. But unfortunately it cannot be said that his books have made exactly the same impression upon non-Catholic historical scholars, and the reason for this is not far to seek. They charge him with using history to serve apologetic aims, and with being a propagandist historian, more interested in defending Catholicism than in the dispassionate presentation of historical truth. The non-Catholic scholar opens one of Mr. Belloc's books and finds that although the author engages in controversial attack he does not cite his authorities; there are no footnote references, and thus, although the book is probably read with pleasure and avid interest, more often than not it is then put aside as of small importance — interesting and provocative, yes, but primarily a piece of Catholic special pleading. It is most unfortunate that this prejudice against Mr. Belloc exists, because it is neither intelligent nor fair; for although Mr. Belloc does indeed make a legitimate use of history to defend the Church against its traducers, he does not distort truth to achieve that end. He reads his authorities and knows them well; he is admirably objective, and a very

dangerous opponent in historical controversy. Moreover he
has the kind of mind that can extract right meaning from
evidence and make the sources yield their full significance;
and it is especially on that account that he is a much better
historian than his more 'scholarly' critics. But it remains
not the less true that his work commonly does not penetrate
with authority into professional historical circles, where
high standards of intellectual neutrality and documentation
are demanded. There he has been labeled, like Macaulay or
von Treitschke, Froude or Janssen, as a propagandist historian, whose books are brilliant pieces of literature 'to be
used with caution.'

Thus it seems very evident that the Catholic historian, if
he is really to 'penetrate,' must not only take great pains to
work comprehensively over all the sources and to document
his studies carefully; he must also abstain scrupulously from
introducing apologetic argument into his work. This is
demonstrated by the high prestige in non-Catholic circles
which attaches to such historians as Pastor, Döllinger,
Duchesne, and Lord Acton, and also by the success which
Christopher Dawson, ablest of our historians of culture, is
rapidly winning for his brilliant books. Despite the fact that
Mr. Dawson is a philosophically minded historian and a
superb Catholic apologist, he conforms admirably to the
highest standard of objectivity and documentation, and
refuses to mix apologetics with historical science. "The
propagandist historian," he has written, "is inspired by
motives of a non-historical order, and tends unconsciously to
falsify history in the interests of apologetics. . . . For the
last century and more there has certainly been a tendency
among Catholic writers to make history a department of
apologetics. . . . Actually this way of writing history de-

feats its own ends, since as soon as the reader becomes suspicious of the impartiality of the historian he discounts the
truth of everything he reads."[4]

Mr. Dawson, of course, is very far from asserting that the
apologist for Catholicism has no right to make use of historical argument; he only insists that the Catholic historian,
when writing strictly as a historian, keep apologetics out of
his work. And this implies a clear recognition that after all
the best historical apologetic for the Faith is the clear, truth-
ful, and objective narration and analysis of the behavior of
men. Let true history speak and the Faith is defended; if
Catholics have been guilty of sin or wrongheadedness, let
the fact be candidly stated; for Catholics are not the Church
and when they dishonor her by wrong acts they only vindicate the divine thing that lives in their despite. The one
effective way of discrediting the history that misrepresents
and traduces the Church is to substitute true history, convincing one's audience by obeying the most exacting canons
of critical scholarship, and even eschewing, as far as possible,
all acrimonious historical controversy.

An admirable example of the right method and spirit
in which to carry on the 'counterattack' is to be seen in
Professor Gustave Constant's recent history of Henry VIII's
schism with Rome. As Mr. Belloc says, in a preface to the
English translation of the work: "The author has read
everything, used everything and checked every date and
name with the most industrious accuracy. It is in the best
tradition of the *oeuvre documentée*." This French Catholic
scholar, erudite and objective, free of all prejudices implanted by British 'official history,' has written a book which
one may confidently expect to penetrate with authority
wherever the sixteenth century is seriously studied. Indeed

---

[4] *The Making of Europe*, p. xviii. Sheed and Ward, publishers.

it is already doing so, although it is perhaps too much to hope that it will actually fill what Augustine Birrell fifty years ago called "the ugliest gap in an Englishman's library . . . which ought to contain, but does not, a history of the Reformation of Religion in his own country." Since then, however, a great deal of careful study has been given to Tudor England by scholarly students, and a first-class account of Henry VIII's breach with Rome is now made possible. Let us see what the story is.

2

M. Constant begins by remarking that "the occasion of the English Schism is so patent and indisputable that many people scarcely trouble to look for the causes, while some even think that the occasion of it, Henry VIII's divorce, was in reality the cause."[5] But if not the divorce, what then was the cause? For an answer to that question we are bidden to consider the previous history of England, the whole state of the times, and the position of the nation, the King, the Church, and the Papacy. Henry's schism, as a contemporary might have judged it, was no more than an episode in the long conflict between Church and State, which in Tudor times was already a very old conflict. It had raged from the Norman conquest to the days of Edward III, and a long series of laws restraining the papal jurisdiction in England had been enacted by Crown and Parliament; which laws were a "source of inspiration" at the time of the schism.

The Church of Augustine and Theodore, of Bede and Boniface, of Alfred and Thomas à Becket, from the eleventh century onward had been harassed again and again by a secular power jealous of the pope. Respect for the Papacy

---

[5] *The Reformation in England*, p. 1. Sheed and Ward, publishers.

had then gradually declined in the "period of moral corruption and confusion" which set in with the Avignon residence, continued through the Great Schism and conciliar movement, and culminated in the Renaissance disorders and Italian wars, "in which the Popes had to take part on equal terms with petty temporal princes, exchanging the tiara for the helmet . . . casting themselves now into the Emperor's arms, now into those of the King of France."[6] This fall of the prestige and moral authority of the Papacy is the most important fact in the whole history of Christendom at the close of the Middle Ages. For so great was this decline that many of the men who cared most about the welfare of religion despaired of the Papacy as the needed instrument of reform; and nothing could have been more ominous for the integrity of the Church Universal, representing as it did the one vital principle of unity among restless and growing nations. In previous ages all great Church reformers had rallied to the pope, placing their faith in him as the only possible agent of general reform. But now that faith was failing, and how could it have been otherwise? The Papacy was no longer strong; relatively it was weak, very weak; and of course this weakness was the reason why there existed so much open corruption in the clerical body with consequent damage to the religious education of Christendom.

Every age of papal misfortune has been also an age of misfortune for the whole Church. Mr. Chesterton hit the nail on the head when he said that although the Reformation is commonly called a protest against the power of the pope, it should rather be described as a protest against the impotence of the pope. Constant shows this central historical truth about the age of the Reformation very clearly.

---

[6] *Ibid.,* p. 4.

English affection for the Holy See had cooled to the same extent that the English clergy had deteriorated and the English Church been enslaved to the monarchy. What indeed could the pope have done to remedy the sorry state of the spiritual order in England? "Since Henry VII's day a bishop had become a royal official drawing a pension from the Church's revenues; his cleverness had brought him to the king's notice, and he looked to the latter for preferment. . . . His own see never saw him, except when he was worn out, aged, or in disgrace. . . . In 1530 all the episcopal sees save four belonged to non-residents or royal officials. The same could be said of half the deaneries and archdeaneries. All these men were better qualified to serve the state than the Church. All they desired from the latter was an income; they thought little of honouring her by their virtues. They were all ready for servitude, and so Henry VIII's task was simplified." Therein lies the chief reason for that bitter anticlerical feeling which was displayed by an influential part of the population and became so rampant in the House of Commons, recruited as this body was from the gentry and rich merchant classes. These elements, M. Constant writes, "upheld Henry VIII's policy as much as any royal official would have done. . . . All Henry had to do was to fan the passions of Parliament. . . . There was no need to enslave it, he simply let it have the reigns. . . . Parliament was aiming less at Rome than at the Church, whose privileges it hated and whose property it envied, but in striking at one it hit the other."[7]

Such were the basic causes of England's break from Rome, although to set them forth is not to minimize the guilt of a king who wanted a divorce and had an appetite

[7] *Ibid.*, pp. 19, 20, 31, 32.

for tyranny. Henry could have been a powerful agent for a right Church reform — might indeed have been a great Catholic prince, for the requisite qualities were his — had he not chosen instead to turn "the needs of his people, their passions and grievances, and even their national spirit," to serve his own personal desires. There was no irresistible compulsive force driving the 'Defender of the Faith' to commit the fateful schismatic act. He could have chosen otherwise, and nothing proves this more convincingly than the fact that although the attack on the clerical order won considerable applause, the rupture with Rome was accepted by the English nation with virtual indifference. Only a few men seemed to care greatly; the martyrdom of St. Thomas More and St. John Fisher for the cause of Roman unity was unique; England's defection was "general, absolute, and complete"; it was almost unopposed, and yet there was no exultant sense of national liberation. The nation did not rush enthusiastically into schism; it simply accepted schism, as if the matter were of no very great importance. So severe was the papal tyranny under which the English had groaned!

Orthodox though he was to the end of his days, and ardent in his Catholic devotional life, it was not possible for Henry to bring to full stop a movement which had substituted the royal supremacy for the papal obedience. His secretary, Thomas Cromwell, whose ideal of government was the sacred despotism of the Grand Turk, urged him on with the tempting bait of wealth and power, and so the great spoliation of the monasteries quickly came to pass. But this was really inevitable, once the schism had been consummated; for there is a character of universality — a supreme dedication to ends that go beyond prince, nation, and world — in monasticism, which does not accord well with national churches, and it would have been hard to keep a place for it in the nationalized English Church. For a thousand years the monks had been the militia of the popes, and it was not safe to permit them a corporate survival. The monasteries were indeed regarded "as smouldering fires which might well be expected to conceal the last traces of an attachment to Roman Catholicism."

But even the suppression of the monasteries, revolutionary as it was in ultimate results, was not without precedents that made easy the way of the despoilers. The alien priories had been robbed in the thirteenth and fourteenth centuries, and suppressed in the fifteenth. "At a later date the Pope allowed certain religious houses in England to be suppressed so that their income might be used for the building of colleges and hospitals." Wolsey, as Papal Legate and Lord Chancellor (foreshadowing the coming union of spiritual and temporal authority), had suppressed monasteries right and left, dissolving twenty-nine houses in the southern counties between 1524 and 1528. He is said to have contemplated confiscation on a larger scale, and M. Constant judges that he "had no more thought for the dispersed religious than Henry VIII afterwards showed." Certainly the agents he employed for the inspection and dissolution of monasteries were scarcely better than the inquisitors employed by the King a few years later. In the complaints to the King against these agents the name of Cromwell was the one most frequently mentioned. "It was his apprenticeship. His master's fall interrupted the work, but he resumed it, on a larger scale, when the king became the 'supreme head of the Church of England' and chose Cromwell for his counsellor."[8]

Was there, then, a corruption in the English monasteries

---

[8] *Ibid.*, p. 147.

which could be pleaded as a reason rather than invented as a pretext for their dissolution? M. Constant does not dwell much upon the old accusations which no historian today any longer repeats, now that Blunt, Dixon, Gairdner, and Gasquet have written. But he does say "it cannot be denied that the English monasteries, like many others elsewhere, stood in need of a certain reform," and "the almost universal defection of the religious at the time of the schism proves better than anything else that they had lost their first fervor." In monastic circles at least it might have been expected that Henry's breach with Rome would have been vigorously opposed, but it was not so.[9] Yes, there was undoubtedly a great need of reform, but dissolution was not reform, and if some people today (Mr. G. G. Coulton for example) still insist rather irrelevantly on the faults of religious persons, no one can maintain that these were anything but pretexts for what the King and Cromwell did. The actual reason was quite something else: "Landlords among the nobility hankered for the monastic properties adjoining their own. Wealthy merchants longed to have estates in the country that they might become gentlemen. None of these men any longer understood the ideals, the religious enthusiasm, or the Christian sentiments which caused the medieval barons to build or endow abbeys. For over a century (1399–1509) not more than eight religious houses had been founded. It seemed to the *nouveaux riches* that no useful service was served by these houses. . . . Men understand least that which they most lack. . . . The idea of suppressing the monasteries harmonized therefore with the principles of the governing classes. . . . The task of estab-

---

[9] The best recent study is Geoffrey Baskerville's *English Monks and the Suppression of the Monasteries* (Yale University Press, 1937). He makes it luminously clear that the bad state of the religious houses was due directly to the weight of domination and exploitation put upon them by the lay nobility and gentry.

lishing the royal supremacy had been achieved. But it was necessary to secure as firm supporters of the new regime the classes whose parliamentary representatives had helped to found it. Only in this way could any reactionary movements, after the king's death, be foiled. . . . The dissolution of the monasteries was in fact, and was probably intended to be, a gigantic bribe designed to bind the most influential classes of English society indissolubly to the religious revolution."[10]

After relating the history of the schism and the suppression of the monasteries, M. Constant goes on to present four careful studies of the champions of Catholic unity, the advanced party in the schism, the moderate party, and the dogma of the Church of England. The first of these has to do with the opposition to Henry offered by the sainted martyrs, More and Fisher, and the tireless efforts of Cardinal Pole to close the schism with Rome. The second is a treatise on Cranmer, Cromwell, and the party of Lutheran tendency which only the King's determined orthodoxy prevented from immediately introducing continental heresy into Anglican doctrine. The last has to do with the retention of that doctrine until the succession of the next ruler, Edward VI.

It is the third of these, the study of the moderate party, which has special value in making the English break from Rome historically explicable. For it is here that we meet the intellectual leaders of the schismatic church, who, although extremely important figures, are less known than More or Fisher, Cranmer or Cromwell. Yet they played a much greater part than is commonly attributed to them. "The majority," observes M. Constant, "forget to study this party, to bring out its salient features, or to reveal the motives behind it, and thus leave in the background one of the most

---

[10] *The Reformation in England*, pp. 151, 152.

characteristic traits of the Reformation under Henry VIII, a trait without which we should but ill understand what the Reformation really was."[11] The men of this party have been called Henricians, and they bore three distinguishing marks: first, they favored the King's divorce; second, they supported the royal supremacy in the church; third, they maintained Catholic dogma against Protestant heresy. Their leaders were four bishops, Gardiner of Winchester, Stokesley of London, Bonner of Hereford and London, and Tunstall of Durham, none of whom can be called a mere obsequious courtier cleric. Constant pronounces them "worthy men" whose talents, learning, and qualities of all kinds attracted the attention of Wolsey, who was a good judge of men, and also qualified them for episcopal honors. The position they took up on the question of the schism was best set forth in Gardiner's *De vera obedientia,* and I believe that therein one may find explanation for the ease with which the King detached England from the papal obedience.

"How absurd," wrote Gardiner, "to say that a certain man, *qua* John is a subject of the prince who is head of the country, but that the same man, *qua* Christian, is no longer a subject of the king! He belongs to the country because he lives in England, and since he is a Christian, he belongs to the Church of England. *But* (italics mine) *what is the Church of England, save an assembly of men and women, of Churchmen and laymen, united in the profession of the Christian religion? To say that the prince is head of the realm but not of the Church would be to make him head of infidels."*

That a leading luminary of the Church, the Bishop of Winchester, could write that passage, tells us more than many learned volumes might tell of the kind of ecclesias-

---

[11] *Op. cit.,* p. 341.

tical mind which accepted and approved the Henrician
reform. Gardiner implies an identity between the Church
of England and the English nation. The concept of the
Church as an independent, autonomous society was apparently alien to his mind, even as it was to Martin Luther's
mind. He had instead the old idea possessed by Caesaro-
papist Byzantines and by the exponents of territorial
churches in the early Middle Ages, against whom St. Boniface and Gregory II, in the eighth century, and St. Gregory
VII, in the eleventh century, had fought. Unless the Church
is what these latter held it to be, namely, an autonomous
order, then the kings and magistrates of this world may
rightly enough claim supreme power over it. Men who held
to Gardiner's doctrine might wish to keep a national Church
in communion with Rome; they might recognize the pri-
macy of the Bishop of Rome in rank and honor, as indeed
Gardiner and the other Henrician prelates did; but they had
no intellectual argument with which to combat the royal
supremacy. And so the Henricians made their submission,
which, as M. Constant states, "did more to establish the
royal supremacy than the execution of Fisher and More."
For they set the doctrine for the whole land, and "faced
with examples such as these, the confusion of the public
conscience can be easily understood. How many people must
have repeated to themselves the words of Lady More to her
husband: Why not do 'as all the bishops and best learned of
this realm hath done'?"[12]

Apart from this erroneous confusion of Church and
nation (which witnesses to the weakness of English philosophy), the Henricians were entirely orthodox, and with the
king in their support they kept the official religious doctrine
of England uncontaminated by heresy until the next reign.

---

[12] *Op. cit.*, p. 363.

But they made the same mistake in religion that the King made in politics. For just as the King, to make himself tyrannically strong, raised up a class of millionaires who a hundred years later destroyed the English monarchy, so the prelates, by cutting loose from the rock of Peter launched the English Church upon the stormy sea of Protestant heresy. Perhaps they may be pardoned for believing that orthodoxy, cut off from Rome, can live, but the conspicuous failure of their experiment should stand as a warning for all future time.

Two great truths are to be discerned in England's Reformation experience which began in schismatic orthodoxy under the rule of a king, and they are truths relevant to great issues facing the world today. The first is that the prince who lays his hand upon the things that are not Caesar's destroys the foundation of his own throne. And the second is that when a branch is cut from the tree that was sprung from the mustard seed it loses the sap of its life and cannot but wither and die.

9

THE PROPERTY BASIS OF LIBERTY

BETWEEN the words *liberty* and *freedom,* as used in this essay, there is an important difference. Liberty denotes that set of conditions or circumstances wherein a person may act from choice, as it pleases that person — the sphere of unconstrained action, in which one meets with no external compulsions or prohibitions. Freedom, on the other hand, is a subjective conception. It designates a consciousness in us of what we are, an inner illumination of our nature whereby we know ourselves as moral agents, able to discern right and wrong and to exercise the power of moral choice. In this sense no man is free who does not know himself as a being possessed of free will. Our Lord, it will be remembered, did not say the truth would set us at liberty, but that it would make us free. For liberty may be conferred from without, as a slave is emancipated or a prisoner discharged, but freedom can be had only by men who know what kind of creatures God fashioned them to be.

Now the reason for making this distinction of word meanings should, I think, be readily obvious. For it is this: there must not be any suggestion here that property ownership, which can secure men against tyranny in the State, is a generative cause of that self-knowledge which is freedom.

The roots of freedom are in the spiritual order, not in the social-economic system; and it would be quite erroneous to fancy that any restoration of diffused property ownership could of itself effect the return of the spirit of freedom which was the mark of our society in its Christian past. That spirit will return when our religion returns; nothing else can bring it back. Indeed, any belief that such a result could issue merely from a rearranged property system would imply acceptance of one of the characteristic falsehoods of positivist and Marxian sociology.

Let it, then, be clear that the question here has to do with the sphere within which members of the human community can act from choice instead of compulsion, and concerns the relationship, if there be any, between such a sphere of un-constrained action and the private ownership of property. That is the one question to be explored, although I shall touch also upon such cognate matters as the rational argu-ment for private property (as distinct from the pragmatic argument), and the necessity of a revived consciousness of freedom if our society is to become again a society of owners.

I

We proceed then to a discussion of the question, bearing well in mind that property ownership means the ownership of productive property, not mere title to one's house in a city block, nor to the clothes on one's back, nor even to dividend shares in an enterprise over which one has no directive control. All these are certainly forms of property, but our discussion here is of the private ownership and control (by real persons rather than fictitiously personal corporations) of the means of production. Now what has that to do with liberty?

Communists and socialists tell us, of course, that it is flatly opposed to liberty. They say there can be no real liberty for men until all privately owned productive property has been abolished; and some such notion seems vaguely present also in the minds of many modern 'liberals' who talk thickly about the 'conflict between property rights and human rights.' But when such people talk of property they are usually contemplating the proletarian scene and the big corporate properties of industrial capitalism; and it is significant that they talk much more of the exploitation than of the enslavement of human beings. For their case against the present order is not so much that the masters of capitalism repress the free action of men as that the rich drive too hard a bargain with the poor.

Indeed, when these people of the Left use the word *liberty* they do so loosely, not meaning the condition in which human beings may act from independent choice, and in matters of the highest human importance, but meaning rather an increase of leisure and consumable goods for the masses. The real crime which industrial capitalism has done against liberty; namely, the destruction of its economic basis in diffused property ownership, they do not seem to resent at all. They talk of higher wages and shorter hours, of nationalizing this and that instrument of production, of various forms of social insurance, of better housing provided by the State, of increased social services — yes, of 'the more abundant life' — but they do not talk much of liberty, unless it be to use that noble word in the sense of the political right to agitate publicly for these servile ends. For the truth is that the objective of nearly all this collectivist striving is

not a liberty suitable to men of free will, but a smoothly
operating economic mechanism for the satisfaction of unlimited material appetites.

To such a pass has come the great movement for human
liberty begun a century and a half ago. The effort to restore
the Republic (that public thing which is distinguished from
the private thing, and also from the royal thing) gradually
becomes an effort to create the Soviet, which may be defined
as what results when the public thing swallows all private
things; when it strips men of all but their status of citizenship and then degrades that status; when it standardizes
and isolates men, defenseless before public power; when it
transforms a hierarchical federation of personal, family, and
group autonomies into a single mass community. How great
has been our fall from the old republican idealism! The
liberals of an earlier day who fought and shed blood for
liberty, knowing what it is and why men should have it,
and affirming a creed of natural rights upon which no
power could trample lawfully — these liberals have passed
away. And in their wake have come their epigones, men of
a different creed or of no creed at all, men who commonly
equate liberalism with the most unprincipled kind of sociological adventuring.

2

The old liberals who brought back the Republic knew
very well the meaning and social-political value of property.
They knew where lay the economic bases of the liberty they
desired to establish. The French of 1789 wrote into their
Declaration of the Rights of Man and of the Citizen that
"property is an inviolable and sacred right." The Virginia

Bill of Rights put "the means of acquiring and possessing property" at the "base and foundation of government." The Massachusetts Bill of Rights contained the same declaration in substance, and indeed all the documents of the early Liberalism reflect a clear awareness of the close bearing of the doctrine of liberty on the doctrine of property. The sociological thought of this Liberalism, best exemplified perhaps in the ideas of Jefferson and Condorcet, was what may be called distributist today, in that it envisaged a widely diffused ownership of the means of production as one of the surest guarantees against all forms of human tyranny. And it is a historical fact (deeply significant but often forgotten by social theorists of our day) that wherever the republican liberating movement swept, it tore landlord feudalism and economic monopoly to pieces and left standing a society of citizen owners.

It was, I think, one of the great misfortunes of our history that the fruits of this victory were not adequately guarded by a competent political power; in other words, that the Liberal State lacked the power to defend the new social order. The old liberals, having won a hard battle against royal absolutism, were suspicious of all strong government and held to the view that the best government is the least government; which is not a truth, but a half truth, and exactly the kind of half truth that goes down with men who neither reflect upon human nature nor have understanding of the organic relation between the social order and the State. The whole and therefore the real truth is not that the least government is the best government, but that the best society will need the least political coercion. The State is a reflex of the social order; it is not the other way round. To say of the State what Jefferson said is not to utter a uni-

versal and timeless truth, but simply to voice a political
opinion which takes for granted the existence of a society
of free, independent, and just human beings.

So that the old liberal political doctrine was only as valid
as the old liberal concept of human nature. Hence it was
that even as the old authoritarian regimes, despising man
greatly, expected too little of him, the revolutionary rebels,
praising man unduly, expected too much of him. They
fancied it was in his nature to be good if given liberty, and
that a free social order would require little policing. They
did not realize at all that the social order of distributive
property, unless guarded by competent public power, would
be disrupted by competitive greed working through industrial and financial capitalism. But that, as we know, is what
happened, and it has brought about today, over vast areas of
the West, a society of big business and proletarianism, in
which for an increasing majority of men the hope and
desire for property — even the very concept of property —
have nearly vanished. Such is the position, indeed, that a
defense of property today is more likely to be received as a
capitalist tract against Socialism than as a plea for the rights
of man.

Now all this change in the social-economic order has
been accompanied by the decline of liberty, that is, by the
return of enormous power exercised by some men over
others. I do not refer to the despotic strait jackets fastened
upon men by political dictatorships (although that is part
of the picture), but rather to the power of employers, landlords, bankers, bureaucrats, politicians, trade-union leaders,
and the like, to restrict the area in which human beings
may act from choice instead of compulsion. There is everywhere a vast increase in the organizing of men, and the organizing does not result from the volition of the organized

but is imposed on these by others. Compulsory disciplines
and — if I may use the much prostituted word — regimenta-
tion of human beings by political and economic powers
grow from year to year; and although much of it is necessary if contemporary civilization is to be spared violent
disaster, and some of it is in fact salutary and eminently
desirable, the net effect of all of it is to narrow the bounds
of liberty.

3

Surely it must be agreed that this is so. I know that many
who profess not to despise liberty regard its decline as the
price we must pay for 'progress'; perhaps it is; I do not
question here the necessity or wisdom of the payment. But
if it be said that there has been no actual decline of liberty,
but only a substitution of one kind of liberty for another,
and that this is shown by the fact that you hear no great
outcry against vanishing liberty, such a statement must be
denied as false. For the evidence of failing liberty is not to
be refuted by urging that men would surely complain of it.
As a matter of fact, one hears discouragingly little grum-
bling of the sort; probably, a vast number do not care about
the matter. For men do not always prize liberty; they may
or may not, depending upon their ultimate desires. There
have been contented slaves, and there have been people with
liberty but little apparent happiness; for liberty is a weighty
and sobering responsibility, suited to the dignity of man but
not always conducive to his joy.

No, you cannot argue rightly that liberty survives because
so few experience any pain in its passing, for the spirit of
servility has grown among us and it is a drug to deaden that
pain. Whoever looks with critical eye at the character of

modern society, wherever this has been made over by
industrial capitalism, will note the spread of all that is
characteristic of servile men: distaste for responsibility,
preference of pleasure and material comforts to personal
independence, a debased concept of human nature, a great
weakening of the will and a sharp decline of voluntary
associational activity. With all this goes a far-reaching decay
of genuinely private life, a great dissolution of the private
sovereignties of home and family, in which human beings
are formed and may come to know themselves in security
and moral freedom.

And there is the additional fact, equally obvious, that the
masses no longer display that multiplicity in taste and
action which results from the exercise of choice; standard-
ization sets in steadily, in all departments of life; and this is
most intimately connected with the loss of the economic
bases of liberty. For as Hilaire Belloc has recently written,
"Deprived of economic freedom, the family, and in some
degree the individual, lack the power to express that diver-
sity which is life. In the absence of economic freedom there
must weigh upon any human society a dead and mechanical uniformity, increasingly laden, and heavy, and stifling,
in proportion to the absence of freedom." One has but to
look at houses, furniture, clothes, popular literature and
amusements, and numerous other aspects of the culture of
the masses, to note how striking this mark has become in
contemporary western society. Throughout all history it has
been the sign of the decay of liberty.

Now there is a very clear and simple reason why the old
distributive property system and liberty arose, flourished and
declined apace in our civilization. So obvious is it indeed
that one would hardly bother to state it, were it not for the
fact that so many persons appear either to have forgotten it

or never to have grasped it at all. And it is that concentrated
ownership of the means of production, whether in the State
or in a few rich men, must make wage slaves of the great
majority of men. They may be well-paid slaves, they may be
housed and fed a great deal better than other men possessed
of liberty; but they have not the power to order their own
lives save on sufferance from their masters. They cannot
oppose their will to those who own and control the means
of production without risk of their livelihood; they cannot
maintain the balance of forces which is required if there is to
be liberty in the social order; they cannot act in self-defense
without resorting to revolution in the State. In short, they
cannot stand on their own, because they own nothing on
which to stand.

All this was perfectly clear to the liberals of a century ago,
as it is obvious to clear-headed Communists today; but it is
not obvious to the sociological adventurers who (without
the slightest regard for first principles in social politics) hail
every new step toward servile collective security as an increase of 'liberty' for the masses. These people indeed either
have never thought at all about the significance of well-
divided property, or when confronted with what seems to
them an odd reactionary notion, fail to understand it. Thus
my collectivist opponent in a recent debate sought to refute
the property argument for liberty by citing this and that
person, present in the hall, who did not own property but
yet enjoyed liberty; which proved no more than that he had
not understood the distributist thesis. For it does not follow
from that thesis that each person, nor even each family,
cannot have liberty without owning some part of the means
of production. The point is not that if you would be free
you must own, but that you must belong to a community
wherein ownership is widely diffused, and wherein, on that

account, a genuine citizenship and an honest public opinion can flourish. In such a community there will be liberty, for the units of society will be able to react against one another, against the State and against monopoly; but that everyone in the State must be an owner of some productive property is obviously an unreal and inhuman conception. "The proprietary (or distributist) State [to quote Mr. Belloc once more] neither can nor should be complete; for it cannot of its nature be mechanical. There will be many comparatively poor, and some comparatively rich. There will presumably be some proportion of dispossessed. But property, and its accompaniment, economic freedom, will be the mark of society as a whole."[1]

4

There are, I believe, encouraging signs today of a clearer recognition of the necessity for maintaining and restoring well-divided property if liberty is to remain a mark of American society. Our own part of the western world has undoubtedly been much disrupted by industrial and finance capitalism and its accompaniment, proletarianism, but a large section of the population retains the sense of ownership and the desire to own and continue to own. There can be, surely, little doubt that among the millions who voted for Mr. Roosevelt in 1936 (to say nothing of those who did not!) there were many who did so not because the so-called New Deal is in part collectivist, but in the hope that its ultimate effect may be exactly the opposite. The President's own ideal vision of America was revealed very clearly in his campaign addresses, in which one heard the distributist note sounded quite distinctly. The property question indeed was

[1] *The Restoration of Property*, pp. 32, 33. Sheed and Ward, publishers.

much discussed (although not very luminously) in the 1936 campaign, and the prospect is that the debate will continue and will attain greater clarity. Nothing, in fact, has been coming more to the front at this time than the matter of property rights, and it may be that out of the vague and muddled discussion of quasi-property rights for workers in their jobs in corporate industry will come some new adaptation of the property institution to large-scale industrial enterprise; although the ultimate objective of distributist striving should be rather the decentralization of industry in small, personally owned units. At any rate it is a healthy sign that more thought is being given today to the social and political importance of property.

Such a prospect offers hope to those who value liberty enough to reflect upon what it is, what its foundations are, and how these may be preserved against the collectivist and servile drift of contemporary society. For it promises some further lifting of the fog of pragmatism that has lain upon our minds and some discovery of where lie the sources of many values which we may still prize greatly but yet are in danger of losing, because, forgetting how we came by them, we have thoughtlessly allowed the basis upon which they rest to weaken.

If this clearing of minds does indeed come about, we shall find that more is required than a few New Deal measures to preserve and restore the property basis of liberty. We shall find that a return to rational philosophy also is called for, because it will not do merely to justify property with the pragmatic argument that liberty requires it as a basis. The right intellectual argument here is not a Benthamite sophistry, but an appeal to nature and reason. I mean that if we would make the case for property a really valid one we must say, as Pope Leo XIII said, that "when man spends the industry of his mind and the strength of his body in procuring the fruits of nature, by that act he makes his own that portion of nature's field, which he cultivates — that portion on which he leaves, as it were, the impress of his own personality; and it cannot but be just that he should possess that portion as his own and should have a right to keep it without molestation." That is the real case for private property, and it would be valid even if well-divided ownership actually worked against liberty.

But the most important truth to be found and brought to light is that property will neither be kept nor restored unless men desire and will that it should be so, and that almost nothing, therefore, can be done toward this end without a change in the spiritual order. All mechanical revolutionary schemes for redistributing ownership must fail unless that change takes place, for you cannot make owners of men who do not want the responsibility of owning. Precisely as communist collectivism and the capitalist collectivism of the Servile State require the extinction of the traditional man, who cared deeply about property and the liberty which it secures, so does a distributist society call for his restoration. And that brings us back to what was said at the beginning of this essay when I made distinction between liberty and freedom. There cannot be a society of owners unless there be a desire for liberty, and there cannot be any strong desire for liberty without a restored consciousness of freedom. Men must know themselves for what they are, and for what end they were fashioned, if they are to keep or to have again that knowledge of freedom which externalizes itself in liberty.

This is a truth which even the old liberals, with all their love of liberty, for the most part did not know. They were fired by a vision that could come only to men of the Christian West, but they did not know how they had come to be the kind of men who could have such a vision. We who have witnessed so great a ruination of their work have little excuse for not seeing what they missed.

10

THE CHURCH AND THE TOTALITARIAN STATE

THROUGHOUT the political communities of the West there appears today a tendency to bring nearly every sphere of human activity — in its social aspect at least — under some form of public or state direction. The trend has been manifest now for several generations, ever since, that is, the old liberalism of the last century began to undergo metamorphosis into a kind of pragmatic socialism. We have had an enormous growth of government, an ever-widening legislative and bureaucratic intervention in the general economic and cultural life of the national community.

No cessation of this trend is in sight, and it would be, I think, unintelligently reactionary to protest that the development is necessarily bad or deplorable, since no one can reasonably doubt that it meets many of the very urgent needs of the age. A big and highly functionalized society demands a big and highly functionalized state. National communities which a few generations ago were mere regional federations in their social-economic aspect have been knit together closely by ties of interdependent economic necessity; and national governments and national administrative controls have had to respond to that transformation. So that, insofar as we have been getting more government because the changing nature of the social order requires it, this growth of the State is no more to be regretted than pure-food laws, marketing acts, or traffic regulations. Without doubt there is danger in it, as in all bold human venturing. There is the danger of multiplying public services beyond the limits at which reasonable tax revenues can support them; and there is also the danger that men of a wrong philosophy may use the vast mechanism of the modern State to devour rightful human liberties. But for so long as a people can retain well-divided property in the means of production and hold fast to the principle of constitutional limitation on the power of the State, there is surely no reason why they should not have as many government bureaus and collective community enterprises as they desire and can reasonably afford.

Such State interventionism, however wide may be the area of its reach, is not to be equated with the political manifestation that is called today the totalitarian State; nor does it lead logically and irresistibly to State totalitarianism. It can undoubtedly lead to bankruptcy of the State, with resultant political breakdown, and hence to crises that may be exploited successfully by politicians bent on setting up a totalitarian regime. But it does not contain in itself the embryo of such a State.

What, then, is the nature of this totalitarian State? What is its distinguishing mark? In this essay I shall seek to answer that question and also two others, which are: How does this new totalitarianism affect the position and activity of the Church? And is the doctrinal basis of such a State acceptable to reasonable men?

I

Many persons have used this rather odd political term to designate the State of unlimited jurisdiction, which rules or may legitimately rule every sphere of human activity: economic, intellectual, and religious expression, education, association, family, matrimony, all cultural activities — these being so ruled that their very existence would seem to depend on sufferance from the civil-political power. Such a State recognizes no rights of man derivative from God and nature and hence outside the bounds of its jurisdiction. No matter what form it may present (democratic, oligarchical, monarchical), it is absolute and may do whatever it wills; it does not exist for the individual and the family, but these exist for it.

Now, so far as it goes, this account of the totalitarian State is correct, but it does not set out in clear light the thing that is worrying Catholics and all other persons today who still recognize the existence of imprescriptible human rights. And why this is so becomes evident quickly when we apply the definition to some of the contemporary States of the world.

Doing that, we find, of course, that the American Republic with its federal structure and constitutional limitations is clearly not totalitarian; but the Russian Soviet is. There the State is not conceived as a permanently necessary institution set up by society for the defense of justice, human rights, and the common good, but as a revolutionary instrument for effectuating the will of the proletariat; which will is an absolute. Such is the orthodox Marxian doctrine of the State (a weapon of the class struggle), and although it may be that Stalin is now getting rid of Marxism by calling it Trotzkyism, there has been no abjuring of this political theory, still less any retreat from the totalitarian absolutism that it legitimizes.

Equally totalitarian is the Japanese State, since it is a sacred monarchy after the immemorial fashion of the East. The ruler is a god, and where the ruler is a god the authority of the State knows no limits; for ordinary human mortals can hardly have rights against deity. Such a State may govern justly and humanely; it may borrow a parliamentary window dressing from western liberalism; but unless it changes the sanction of its authority it cannot be other than totalitarian.

So far, then, this definition serves well enough for bringing into relief essential differences of nature in political authorities. But when you apply it to other States you find that some which are commonly thought to be friendly to a proper human liberty, and are considered 'liberal' States, are also totalitarian, formally so at least. Thus England, although generally regarded as a land of much liberty, has had a totalitarian State ever since the national secession from the Catholic Church; for the English crown has never made a concordat with Rome, nor have the British people ever accomplished a revolution affirming the natural rights of man. No doubt the traditional disposition of the State has been of tolerance and little interference with private spheres of activity; but the State, or crown authority, as exercised by Parliament, is absolute and unlimited. There are no constitutional limits on legislative jurisdiction, and it would be perfectly lawful to introduce a complete communism or abolish the Mass again provided all were done by a properly drawn Act of Parliament.

Very much the same general statement may be made of the present-day French State, despite the fact that the

French are still largely Catholic and were the first European people to put a declaration of human rights into organic law. The supreme power in France today is a parliament with no constitutional bounds upon its jurisdictional competence; so that France also is formally totalitarian, and has been ever since the Republic broke its Concordat with the Vatican in 1905.

When, however, one turns to Nazi Germany and Fascist Italy, where the words *totalitarian State* first appeared and are chiefly used, one finds that these States, although proclaiming themselves to be totalitarian, are really not so, or at least not according to the definition we have here been testing. For each has made a concordat with the Papacy, and by so doing has recognized in its law a limit upon the reach of its authority.

From these facts I think it should be evident that the definition of the totalitarian State as the State of unlimited legislative prerogative does not really tell us very much, and that we cannot get very near to grasping the thing that worries us today by merely examining abstract political forms. That is to say, only an external account of the totalitarian State is given in this definition; for the substance of the thing we must probe into what has transpired in those political communities which find themselves subjected to totalitarian regimes. Let us do that briefly, taking first the case of Russia.

Unlimited political absolutism was not, of course, first introduced into that unfortunate country by the Communist Party politicians. They simply changed its sanction and expanded its administrative and police activities. The old Czarist regime was sacred monarchy after the model of Byzantine Caesaro-papism; that of the Soviets takes its character from the Marxian ideology of the 1917 revolution.

That momentous upheaval was an attempt at much more than a far-reaching social readjustment in behalf of the poor and disinherited, more even than the extermination of a ruling and exploiting class. It aimed at nothing less that the abolition of one culture and the creation of a new one; it was truly radical, for it struck at the roots of the old order; it sought to tear humanity loose from one kind of soil and to transplant it in another. What was wanted was a new kind of man altogether different from traditional Christian man: an atheistic man with a radically altered vision of reality and conception of human nature and destiny. The Russian revolution was thus primarily a religious revolution, and its most significant work was not the overthrow of feudalism, capitalism, and imperialism, but of Christian Orthodoxy. The central event was the enthronement of a new god by the deification of proletarian humanity, whose shrine is the machine, whose revealed truth is dialectic materialism. And this new god was a jealous god, even as the true God is jealous; it would have not part of a man but the whole man; not a partial, relative, and conditional allegiance, but a full, absolute, and unconditional allegiance. It was, in short, a totalitarian god and the instrument of its power has been correspondingly totalitarian.

Russia offers us, in fact, a good and clear illustration of the general truth that every totalitarian regime is based upon some religious theory affirmed or implied. That of the Byzantine Empire and old Holy Russia, as also of Tudor England, issued from the corrupting union of schismatic Christianity with prince worship; and that of the first French Republic was produced by the eighteenth-century religion of Nature and Reason. There has never existed — nor indeed could there exist — any political

regime that did not reflect faithfully the religion or condition of religion among the people sustaining the regime.
For the State is a reflex of the society giving rise to it, and
its relation to society is organic; it is an instrument or organ
for the service of whatever ends the community may bend
it to serve. Hence it is that the great hideous reality in
Russia has not been the Communist totalitarian State, but
the false god of proletarianism and machine worship that
has used this organ or instrument with such devastating
terror. Russia has not been afflicted merely by despotic
politicians; she has been made victim of an iniquitous
religion.

Now, in Fascist lands there has been something rather
different, for totalitarianism arose there out of national
rather than class revolutions. Some writers, it is true, hold
this an insignificant difference and take the view that
Bolshevism and Fascism, each manifesting the totalitarian
State, are essentially the same thing. This was the thesis
of Dr. Waldemar Gurian in a book published last year,
wherein he sought to show Russian Communism and
German National Socialism as identical, the Nazis being
merely "brown Bolshevists." Their identity, he said, is to
be seen in their common worship of the social order; that
is, in the affirmation by each that the supreme end of
human activity is the realization of a particular social ideal.
No doubt there is much truth in this thesis, but the
fact that Russia and Germany today tend more and more
toward a common military State socialism ought not to
obscure recognition that ideological differences still retain
a considerable importance. Doubtless the Nordic race or the
German nation is no more a fit object of worship than the
proletariat, but the fact is that the former deity has not yet
exhibited so jealous a disposition as the latter. Or at least

we may say that no Fascist State has yet declared open warfare on paying honor to the Creator of mankind. Moreover, it would be a serious oversight to ignore the deeply differing conceptions of the nature of the State held by Fascists, Nazis, and Communists. Political doctrines are rooted in the moral and spiritual affirmations which, consciously or unconsciously, all peoples make; and we have here no mere empty ideological divergences, but symptoms of opposing visions of reality. The Communists, as I have said above, conceive the State to be in essence a weapon of conflict called into being by the exigencies of the class struggle, which they regard as the main action of history. But for this warfare the State would have no reason for existing; so that when the proletariat no longer needs this weapon of war and terror — when, that is, all other classes throughout the world have been liquidated — the State is to "wither" away in utopian anarchy. This political doctrine (obviously a declaration of war on all non-Communist States) proceeds with the logic of the multiplication table from the philosophy of historical and dialectical materialism; which philosophy dominates Soviet educational and propagandist activity. It has formed the minds of perhaps twenty-five million new human beings, and the ideological word has therefore been made flesh. Doubtless the general line of Soviet philosophy does move away from what I believe is called a pure "mechanicism" and toward a quasi-idealist definition of matter, but suffi- cient reflection will make it clear that this in no way affects the historical philosophy of the class struggle. For the central thesis of Marxism is not that matter is of this or that nature, but that matter (whatever be its nature) exhausts reality. It will not be as easy as some may fancy to convert Marxism into an idealism less at variance with the Christian view of man, the State, and the universe.

Now Fascism radically opposes this Communist doctrine of the State and does so from the depths of its nature. It does not conceive the State as a weapon or instrument to be sloughed off or to wither away, but conceives it as the organizing principle and permanent directing intelligence of the national community, whose proper business is its own development and not the conquest of the world. Signor Mussolini has defined the State as the "juridical incarnation of the nation." He has said: "The people are the body of the State and the State is the spirit of the people. In the Fascist concept the people are the State and the State is the people." And again he has defined the totalitarian State as that which "absorbs into itself, in order to transform and strengthen them, all the interests, all the hopes of a people." The State is thus envisaged as a people fully incorporated, and without such complete incorporation no nation is more than partially constituted.

The words of the Italian Duce quoted here are taken almost at random from his writings and discourses on Fascist doctrine respecting State and nation. Basic in this is the affirmation that the supreme social reality in the historical world of modern times is a mystical spiritual organism, the nation. This alone can infuse value into man's terrestrial life, and therefore may properly command his full and unconditional allegiance. Man is thus not an isolated and autonomous being, not a social atom, but a member of a body: the mystical body of the nation. And his supreme duty on earth is to perform the function assigned to him as a member of that body. The nation is a superpersonal organism and the State is related to it as, in the human body, the soul is related to the physical members. Hence even as in a human being all parts of the body should be under disciplined control of the reason and will, so in a rightly and fully constituted nation all its members must be in obedient and hierarchical co-ordination determined and guided by the State. Such is the theory and practice of the Fascist totalitarian State. And obviously it puts aside as irrelevant all political speculation concerning sovereignty, natural rights, contractual theories of government, and so forth. For the hand is not in contract with the head, nor has the organ rights independent of the organism.

One sees here not only conceptions reminiscent of the early and Platonic Middle Ages, but the ultimate development of the idealist doctrine of nationalism. Fascists boast that it is a new political doctrine, but it is no such thing. J. G. Fichte, chief prophet of modern German nationalism, taught substantially the same doctrine nearly a century and a half ago, when he expounded the thesis that nations are organisms and called for the kind of State that would "apply the whole surplus power of all its citizens, without exception, to the furtherance of its own ends." The Fascist doctrine of the national totalitarian State did not in fact originate in Italy but in Germany. It is the union of Herder's famous thesis that nationalities (*Völker*) are mystical superpersonal organisms (each with its own soul) and the Hegelian doctrine of the State as the embodiment on earth of the Absolute Spirit.

2

Having now set forth the essential character of contemporary totalitarianism, let us turn to the question of how it accords with the life of the Catholic Church.

There is obviously no need on this point to say much of
Communist politics, since no imaginable common ground
exists on which a genuinely Marxian State can come to
peace with the Church. These are irreconcilably opposed,
and for so long as each retains its distinctive character no
resolution of the conflict can even be conceived. To be
sure one can imagine a pragmatic Stalin making a concordat, but were that to come about it would mean that
Russia had at last ceased to be Marxian.

A similar short answer could be given concerning the
Church and the Fascist State if Fascist nationalism had as
yet shown a temper as absolutist as proletarianism; that is,
if Fascists were really worshiping the nation as a deity and
were carrying their doctrine to logical conclusion by bringing religion under the rule of the State. It is true that
Germany, plagued by the political tradition of Lutheranism
and the ugly heresy of racialism, has gone far in this
direction; but I doubt that anyone familiar with contemporary Italy (which as a matter of fact proclaims itself
officially a Catholic State) could say — without rhetorical
exaggeration — that the nation is there paid divine worship.

The essential point is, of course, that both Fascist States
have made concordats with the Church, committing themselves to respect her liberty within a specified sphere, and
so acknowledging in their law that although everything
else may be within the State the Church is not. Thus is
recognition given to her autonomous corporate existence —
a recognition Marxism can never give. It is well known,
of course, that on occasion, and especially in Germany,
politicians have paid scant respect to this commitment.
But supposing it were most scrupulously respected, what
conflict would there be between the Church and this
Fascist totalitarian State? Not any in principle, I believe

we must admit, since the Church has no quarrel with States that respect the independence of her spiritual life and accord to her an agreed-upon sphere of activity in the social community. Moreover, it does not appear that the doctrine of the nation as an organism denies any Catholic dogma. Nor can it be said that there is any distinctly Catholic objection to a very high degree of national organization and discipline.

And yet without doubt this Fascist totalitarianism is not in harmony with either the polity of the Church or the instinct and mentality of people adhering to the Catholic religious tradition. It is not that clashes between secular and spiritual authorities must occur periodically where such political regimes prevail, for all real powers exercised by human beings in this world will clash on occasion. Neither is it that the Catholic mind is disposed to reject the political guardianship over economic and other kinds of secular activity. Still less is it that the Catholic instinct necessarily opposes the inevitable military aspect of the Fascist State. The reason for trouble lies rather in the fact that Fascists tend to regard the Church as being only an abstract and spiritual reality, as having a mere platonic existence; whereas the Church is not a purely spiritual thing, but also a concrete, visible, and even material thing, acting not only in the minds and souls of men, but in the economic and social community as well. It, too, is an organism with an independent historical life, and that life undoubtedly suffers choking constriction in this totalitarian State; even though there be legal recognition, through a concordat, that the Church has a corporate existence separate from the form of the State. The State may indeed profess itself Catholic and officially embrace the Church, as the new Italy has done, but such an embrace is not unlikely to be more

suffocating than convincingly amorous. No doubt all would
go well enough in an ideal Catholic State; that is, in a
political community without dissent, heresy, or atheism;
but no such State has ever existed.

The reason for this lack of concord (in practice if not
in theory) springs, I believe, from the fact that Fascist
totalitarianism is based on the acceptation as real of something which is probably not real at all. And here we come
to the last of the questions raised in this essay: Is the
doctrinal basis of the totalitarian State acceptable to reasonable minds? Communist State theory is, of course, reasonable from the premises of historical materialism, and Fascist
political thought is equally so if nations are in truth organisms. But what reason is there for regarding a nation as
anything other or more mysterious than a historical community of rather like-minded people having a common
tradition and common language, habits, and mental attitudes? The human race is indeed an organism, for it is
a unique species of single origin in our first parents. And
the Church is an organism because it had its genesis in
the New Adam, our Lord Christ, Head of the mystical
body of the baptized. But why should a nation be thought
of as an organism? Without doubt it has an organic character, for it is part of the human race; but surely one can
only call it an organism by leaving the atmosphere of
reason and clearly conceived reality and plunging deep into
the fog of an irrational German mysticism that came down
upon the western world a century and a half ago.

In conclusion here it may be observed that the one
doctrine of the State that involves neither an atheistic
denial of spiritual reality nor submission to the mysticism
of superpersonal national organisms, is the doctrine of the
Republic. Unfortunately, in a world that has so largely

lost its historical memory and faith in the Christian God and therefore is searching to find some substitute absolute, not much thought is given to that sane republicanism which is the common political tradition of Christendom. Most men, indeed, appear to have no notion of what a Republic actually is, fancying vaguely that it is merely a State without a king. The Christian political thinker, however, knows what it is; knows that it is the public thing maintained by a multitude of private 'things,' that it is not an absolute but contingent reality; that it belongs to the community, not the community to it. Only where it is upheld, and by a community which in its turn recognizes a dependence on yet higher powers, can men discharge freely and in reasonable peace their dual duties to Caesar and to God.

11

THE CATHOLIC MIND AND MODERN POLITICS

I

IN THE years following hard upon the close of the Great War, when Bolshevism was still a new thing and the socialist republic in Germany gave some promise of enduring — when, too, our own nation was in reaction from the vigorous rule of Wilson — there was a great deal of talk and writing about the 'passing of politics.' I recall a book bearing that exact title, and it was but part of a considerable literature that explained how and why the western world was moving out of a political age into a technological and sociological age. The political man, according to this view, was becoming obsolete; no longer did he make, nor was he any longer competent to make, the decisions that really mattered in the New Society. The Great War, which had been his blunder, had written his doom, and not again would he have the main direction of affairs. The succession was passing to industrialists, to men of finance, engineers, technicians, economists, and so forth, practical and expert men who would know how to keep the peace and build prosperity.

This belief has a near affinity to Marxian ideology, but it was, nevertheless, vaguely in the minds of many especially here in America who know nothing of Marxism. It lay back of the naïve hope that an 'engineer' would do better than a politician in the Presidency, and it was discernible plainly in all that common talk of government being essentially a business, of the political task being on all fours with that of corporation management. For discredited equally with the political man were all rational principles of politics, all doctrines touching the subject of sovereignty or the *raison d'être* of political power, or having to do with the nature and limits of State authority. Pragmatism reigned supreme in the study of politics and was transforming this again into a mere cameralism or purely descriptive treatment of governmental method.

But how great today is the change from all that! The man of politics has climbed again into the saddle, and the State — the political organ of the community — has risen to greater power than it has ever had in the past. A new leviathan appears in our midst, and all the liberty for which men have fought during the past century and a half seems threatened by a political thing, omnipotent, absolute, and totalitarian. The old-fashioned liberal is aghast at the denial of his creed, the Christian shudders at the return of fierce persecution, and wherever men of tradition gather the ominous thing is discussed.

In this fact lies the reason why a revival of genuine political thinking has now begun, even in America, to dispel in some measure the fog of witless pragmatism that has lain upon our minds. For without any doubt we stand in the presence of a real peril. The fact is generally admitted, and if some are less apprehensive than others, few thoughtful persons would venture to call it a

mere bogey or say there is no reason for alarm. For everyone who knows the trend of modern history and the drift
of the contemporary age recognizes that active State intervention in human affairs has undergone enormous increase
in the last few generations, that this increase has been
much accelerated in our own day, and that indications for
the future point to a great deal more of it to come. Our
whole society and culture, as Mr. Christopher Dawson has
remarked, are rapidly becoming 'politicized.'

Nowhere, of course, was this fact discerned earlier or
more shrewdly than in the Church, which has ever
cautioned men against removing strict limitations from
the temporal power. The Church has had to act warily
and with great prudence, to take new bearings of her
position, considering with special care and caution how
her necessary freedom and independence can be maintained
in the new age; for although to her the problem, in its
essential nature, is not new, never before has it shown
the magnitude and complexity which mark it in the de-
Christianized contemporary world. Never, therefore, has
the need been so great for ecclesiastical statesmen, astute
and able to conduct a policy that can safeguard the essential liberties of the Church without disturbing the peace of
civil society. Hence the extension of the system of concordats and the remarkable patience the Vatican has exercised in all disputes over interpretation of these. Pope Pius
XI concluded such pacts with thirteen states during the
first ten years of his reign, and so large a number indicates
the tortuous way which the Church must take in preserv-
ing her liberty of action against the new social disciplines
which the State is everywhere seeking to impose.

Now all this, fortunately, has made Catholics keenly
aware of the rough seas in which the Church is sailing,

and aroused in us a renewed and encouraging determination to defend the Church against being swallowed by the new leviathan. But it is by no means equally evident that we have as yet shown much disposition to grapple with the high political question of our day. Quick to protest unlawful encroachment of secular power, yes, that we have been (although with small effect); but I doubt if it would be going too far to say that we have been rather inclined to hide the light of our own political thought under a bushel. Briefly, what I mean is this: We have been a little inclined to forget that we are not only Catholics determined to be loyal to the Church, but also full citizens of the modern State; that we do not merely go into civil society to defend there the freedom of the Church, but are born there also, even as in the Church; on which account we have a concern for the civil order (as an autonomous order) quite apart from, and in addition to, our defense of the Church within it. We are native to two societies, religious and civil, and are under a no less obligatory command to render unto Caesar what is Caesar's than to render unto God what is God's; although there have been times (of which the present, I believe, is one) when many of us have remembered the second of these commandments rather more explicitly than the first. That is to say, when Caesar asks for too much we may be tempted to deny him even his rightful due; in which case it can hardly be said that we express perfectly the mind of the Church.

Recall for illustration the events of an age not greatly unlike the present: the persecutions of Roman imperial times. So severe was the distress that some Christians turned from the State as from a cursed and satanic thing. The Apocalypse refers to the Roman power in language of abhorrence, which is rather like the language that has

been poured out in our day against the Communist and
Fascist States. It was the great harlot, the beast drunken
with the blood of the saints and destined to a terrible
chastisement for its crimes. Yet that did not express the
whole Christian mind, for in St. Paul — that admirable
man of sanity — there was discernible a real devotion to
the empire. He would glory only in the Lord Christ, yes,
but he could also refer rather proudly to his Roman
citizenship, and it would seem that he valued highly the
Roman State order as a means, under God, of Christian
propaganda; so that to him the existing civil-political
authority, although grievously misused, was an expression
of the divine will and plan for the human social world.
Leo XIII was but repeating the doctrine of Paul when,
in *Immortale Dei* of 1885, he wrote of God's having
"appointed the charge of the human race between two
powers, the ecclesiastical and the civil, the one being set
over divine, the other over human things. Each in its kind
is supreme, each has fixed limits within which it is contained, limits which are defined by the nature and special
object of the province of each." That is the mind of the
Church in the modern age, and it was the same in the
Church of antiquity, when this doctrine was repeated faithfully by writers of every generation from Nero to Constantine. Concern for upholding the Roman State order
was a mark of the Christian mind; the apologists pointed
repeatedly to it in disproof of the charge that the Church
was hostile to the empire. And after Constantine the
Church became the most powerful support of the imperial
political system.

Now it was wholly consistent with the Catholic character that this should have been so, for the Catholic
character is conservative in the right sense of that word.

It was Catholic society that conserved the best and most valuable things of classical civilization; it is Catholic society that conserves the values of the medieval order. We have been, there is no doubt, the true conservators of tradition in the western world; through us that world has memory, has retained knowledge of its roots. Time and again it has drifted away from traditions that we guard, has therefore turned its face again to us for guidance. It is doing this today in search of rational principles of politics, and the very least reason why we must not fail it is that we ourselves are part of it.

2

But what are we to do? What is the work that calls for execution? It is a work of restoration, of bringing forth anew the common political tradition of our civilization; and I think it may be said that a special responsibility for this work lies upon Catholics of our own country because the American Republic, in which it is our good fortune to have share, without doubt is nearer to being an embodiment of this tradition than any other political community of the contemporary world — save perhaps the Irish State as projected in the new De Valera constitution. One may say this because the substance of this tradition is the monarchical republic, reposing on community sovereignty, respecting natural law, natural rights, and the freedom of the spiritual order, and wielding an authority derivative from a social contract. That tradition was born in antiquity and developed in the Middle Ages, but in modern times largely forgotten. The American Revolution brought its partial restoration; so also did the French; but neither restored the whole of it, and during the past century what of it had been recovered has been fading out again under the blighting influence of political unreason and pragmatism. Not yet to be sure has it gone in our country, but undoubtedly so much has been done to obscure it that if we do not grasp it firmly afresh we may conceivably lose it.

Now the fact of central importance in the whole history of politics over the past five hundred years has been the drift of the modern State from this sane and reasonable political tradition. The drift set in with the breakup of the medieval social order, when the monarchies of Christendom moved from a contractual to an absolutist basis, transformed the common thing (*res publica*) into the royal thing, and began their vast modern usurpation of power. The movement was gradual, never wholly complete of course, and may be dated approximately from the thirteenth to the eighteenth century, or from the age of St. Louis to that of Louis XIV. The turmoil over Protestantism greatly aided it by weakening the position of the Church in civil society and removing the papal bit from the mouths of tyrants; for the change was promoted not least by Catholic princes reaching out for control of the clerical order in their search for new instruments for defense of order, authority, and tradition.

But the point for special note here, and which Catholics who are perplexed by the political question today should remember, is that these late medieval and early modern centuries saw a vigorous stirring of the Catholic mind on the subject of politics, and that the ablest and best representatives of that mind fought a splendid rear-guard action in behalf of the common political tradition of Christendom. Thus Mariana, a monarchist, upheld popular sovereignty and the doctrine that royal power is a grant from the people, even to the extent of legitimizing tyrannicide (an

exaggeration which disfigures his thought); and Cardinal
Bellarmine attacked Calvinistic and aristocratic republicanism in behalf of that type of monarchy which is limited
by law, popular consent, organs of representation, and does
not encroach upon the spiritual domain. Even more fully
was the common tradition set forth and defended in the
political works of the great Suarez: contractual monarchy
derivative from community sovereignty, the subject's obligation to obey his prince and his right to resist princely or
legislative contravention of divine or natural law. This is
the very stuff of the common tradition, from which the
new autocracy and the new antimonarchical republicanism
were both essential deviations. And this is what the Catholic mind advocated in the age which saw a king murdered
in one country and a king worshiped in another.

Now that advocacy, that rear-guard defensive fight, failed
against the force of the modern State with all its jealous
and usurping claims, and for the Church, as for humanity
in general, this was disastrous in the extreme. In some
instances the modern State repudiated the papacy and
created churches under full secular control; in others it
only restricted the independence of the clergy and the pre-
rogatives of the pope. Thus the Tudors persecuted Catholicism in behalf of a nationalized church, while the Haps-
burgs and Bourbons defended it, all the time striving to
bend it to their own political ends. It would be hard to
exaggerate the misfortunes of the Catholic body in that
age which saw the common tradition go down. So heavy
was the attack of anti-Catholic forces that the Church was
virtually compelled to rely upon absolutist Catholic princes
for protection of a minimum liberty to say the Mass and
dispense the sacraments. And that was, I think, the crown-
ing misfortune of all, since now in the minds of many men

(badly instructed but not always of evil will) there arose
the idea of the Church as the mainstay of tyrants. Throne
and altar came to appear as two aspects of one liberty-
destroying thing, and when the revolutionary attack broke
upon the old autocratic order the Church was the target
for the heaviest fire. From having suffered in the State's
embrace she was made victim of its crimes, and that painful experience taught Catholics anew that it is a wrong
policy for the Church to get entangled closely, at any time,
with any State, or to allow herself ever to appear integrally
one with any social-political order. And even were this
not always true, Catholics would have been not the less
right in judging it expedient for the Church to break old
alliances, to go upon her own, and declare to the world
once more her full and absolute autonomy.

This is essentially what was done in the nineteenth century. The Church went into retreat, as it were, that she
might return to the world with fresh energies; as she has
most certainly done in the twentieth century. It is of course
only in a very special and figurative sense that we may say
she went into retreat. The Church did not actually abandon
the world to its headlong rush toward ruin, but she had
much difficulty remaining in it and whenever she spoke
its ears were deaf. For the nineteenth-century states of the
West in which she strove to live and carry on her saving
mission grew steadily more alien to her ways. They became
increasingly indifferent or even hostile to all religion, and
avowedly atheistic groups obtained possession of government even in Catholic countries. More and more, therefore,
the Church was driven back, insulted and bullied by politicians hating not only the Church as a living corporate thing
but also culture and morals informed by the Catholic spirit.
The Church was under persecution in her most ancient

dwelling places during most of the century; even her capital was taken and her chieftain made prisoner by the secularist movement. Dominant political parties nearly everywhere acted on the arrogant assumption that civil power might do what it willed with the clerical order, and it was therefore a quite natural reaction that the old Catholic distrust of the State should rise again to the surface, that many Catholics should think again of the State as the beast drunken with the blood of saints. They were driven back from the world to take sanctuary before the altar and even that was often desecrated. Their work in the world was limited pretty much to the quiet tasks of individual charity and whatever social improvement measures the unfriendly State suffered them to carry on. Hence the Catholic disposition was to abandon the political field to the enemy, and to give the State little thought save what was necessary to avoid its hard grasp. There was little writing by Catholics on political science. We became in a sense aliens in the political order, a kind of strange sect living on in the midst of a new world political religion; and to this, I fear, a great many of us (while remaining theological Catholics) apostatized. Search the political literature of the last century, since let us say de Maistre's time, or take any book treating of modern political thought, and see how many Catholic-minded men are therein discussed. Who does so will be quickly persuaded that we have been little concerned about the political question. And even today, in the splendid Catholic intellectual apostolate to the bewildered western world — expressed in a new historical, philosophical, sociological, and poetic literature — one finds scant treatment of politics. The social problem is extensively, nay wearily, discussed, but not the political problem, not the problem of the State. There are exceptions to this generalization, of course; it is less true of Continental Europe and Ireland than of the lands of English language and culture, and even in these we have such acute political thinkers as Mr. Dawson and Mr. Belloc; but taking us in the large, and especially in America, the generalization will hold.

3

That State which, during the past century, has proved most unfriendly to the Church and suspicious of her members, may be called the Liberal State: the expression in the political order of Liberalism, a movement shot through with destructive doctrines. The worst of these, and that one fundamental to all others, was the simple atheistic doctrine that man is answerable only to himself: that his desire is sovereign and it rather than the laws of God and nature determines the difference between right and wrong. Now, from its nature this Liberalism could not maintain political power on any firm basis, for it could not tolerate any real authority. Because it either denied the authority of God and nature or ignored this as of no political and social importance, it uprooted the sanctions of all human authority. Whence is the authority of the State if it be not from the community? Or how can authority be in the community if the Author of mankind has not placed it there? Or what is man if God has not made him in His image and beholden to His law and judgment? Liberalism was content either to answer these questions with skepticism or to ignore them entirely. Hence it could anchor its State upon no sanctions, could appeal to nothing beyond expediency and material success; and when these began to fail the end of the Liberal State was in sight. Today we are quarreling over the succession.

I mean, of course, no blanket condemnation of all that passed under the name of Liberalism. That movement was not wholly destructive but in part constructive and restorative, many of its most powerful and persistent elements being traditional principles of justice and freedom torn from their proper place in the right hierarchy of moral values. Like Protestantism, Liberalism affirmed a good part of the tradition from which it deviated, and this was plainly not the reason why the Church, over the last century, repeatedly condemned it. Nor was it the reason why the Church showed itself ill at ease with the politics of the movement even when Liberal States were not engaged in open attack on religion. No, the true reason for the Catholic objection to the Liberal State was given by Leo XIII in his encyclical on the Christian Constitution of States, a document which has a claim on our attention today not unequal to that of the great encyclicals on the social question. In it Pope Leo condemned what he termed the 'new jurisprudence' as being 'at variance on many points not only with the Christian but even the natural law.' Among its principles, he said, "the main one lays down that all are equal in the control of their life; that each one is so far his own master as to be in no sense under the rule of another individual; that each one is free to think on any subject just as he may choose, and to do whatever he may like; that no man has any right to rule over other men. In a society grounded upon such maxims, all government is nothing more or less than the will of the people, and the people being under the power of itself alone, is alone its own master. . . . Thus, as is evident, a State becomes nothing but a multitude, which is its own master and ruler. And since the populace is declared to contain within itself the spring-head of all rights and of all power, it follows that the State does not consider itself bound by any kind of duty towards God. . . . The sovereignty of the people . . . and this without any reference to God, is held to reside in the multitude; which is doubtless a doctrine exceedingly well calculated to flatter and inflame many passions, but which lacks all reasonable proof, and all power of insuring public safety and order."

These words, written in 1885, had special reference to those political societies of Europe which were falling into confusion from revolutionary destruction of authority, and the encyclical passed with scant notice among Catholics living in Liberal or quasi-Liberal States wherein the social order retained a reasonable measure of peace. To these Catholics there appeared no pressing need to oppose the 'new jurisprudence' for so long as the social order did not crash; for so long, that is, as the residue of religion and traditional morality restrained men from doing violence to themselves and to the Church. Such a view and policy, however, no longer fit conditions anywhere in the West, for the long-expected and grave crisis has come, and not only in the social-economic but necessarily also in the political order. The Liberal State has failed scandalously and conspicuously as an instrument either for order or for justice, the defense of which is the first duty of all political authority. Hence that Liberal State is passing out from the living western world, is taking on indeed more and more the appearance of a museum piece of nineteenth-century politics.

Something else must therefore come to replace it, and on what that may be depends the fate of human liberty in the temporal sphere. Several alternatives confront us. There is the Communist plan for a totalitarian State absolutism based

on a collectivist economy. Advocates of this are divided in
their strategy, of course; one element seeking to wreck the
existing world and create the conditions for a successful
seizure of the State; the other co-operating with the horde
of social pragmatists and left-wing Liberals to build a huge
quasi-soviet mechanism which may ultimately be utilized
to establish the revolutionary Communist society; but the
goal of both these is the same. A second alternative is the
forcible re-establishment of the dictatorship of the rich
which flourished well before the crisis in capitalism became
too severe for the Liberal State to retain the confidence of
the masses. We would probably be surprised to know how
many there are among us who, having great possessions,
would like to use political power to beat down the enemies
of the rich; certainly we hear voices whispering ominously
that the time for this is drawing near. And then there is
the third alternative, which many would equate with the
second: organic nationalism, the Fascist totalitarian State.
This is powerful and gives many promises of commanding
the future, for it has shown its ability to defeat the Left
while also winning the masses. But it is not an alternative
that Catholics who prize the liberties of the Church will
want to choose.

The fourth alternative is to rally to the defense of the
republic and restore the common tradition. Among those
who perceive and desire this, Catholics, traditionalist by
reason and instinct, as a body are to be found; and they give
to this group a very heavy strength. But many of them have
been slow to acknowledge the reality of the fact of prime
importance in the contemporary social and political world.
That fact is this: because of the complexity and corruption
come about in our society, the traditionalists, even as their
opponents, will have to make a far greater use of political

power than was ever considered needful or legitimate in the past. For as Mr. Dawson has recently remarked, it is "difficult to avoid the conclusion that the movement toward state control in every department of life is a universal one and is not to be confused with the political tenets of a party, whether Communist or Fascist. . . . It rests fundamentally in a perfectly healthy and reasonable desire to put the State and the government of the State above party, and to ensure that the power which has so immense an influence for good or evil in the life of every citizen, shall not be at the mercy of a political clique or the servant of class interests." So great indeed is the area of necessary State action today that whatever group gains possession of the State also takes charge of most agencies for influencing the general cultural life of the community. That, let it be repeated, is the hard fact which many Catholics have been either slow to recognize or hesitant to acknowledge, with resultant hesitancy to admit the supreme importance of having political authority reconstituted by men determined on closing the breach with the common tradition.

A struggle for power is already under way, and there is a real danger that we who are Catholics may let that struggle go by default. Because of our fear of political power there is even the danger that we may drift into tacit alliance with the dying order of political Liberalism; which would be an alliance as unnatural and ultimately disastrous as the alliance which many Catholics once made with the old autocracies. For no greater tactical mistake can be made by a generation of Catholics than to let their religion become confused in men's minds with any social-political order; since if that order fails the Faith will appear involved in the failure. Surely it would be a strange turn of fortune if we, of all people, who opposed the Liberal heresy from the beginning, should be caught in its ruin. Yet that danger is not unreal.

This is not, of course, to imply approval of those Catholic political parties whose disastrous history points so imperious a warning. Reason and experience combine to indicate that confessional politics is a very sure way to bring fresh odium on religion. No, the discussion here has been of Catholics not as members of the Church but as citizens in the political community, having therein, along with their good fellow citizens, a vital concern for a just and rational arrangement of temporal affairs. We are citizens in possession of an ancient treasury of experience and tradition, in which there is much valuable wisdom applicable to the political order of life. Surely there is a duty to bring it forth; not of course as peculiarly Catholic wisdom, since it is not really that at all but only the traditional reason and sanity of our civilization; to which we of the visible Church enjoy special access only because we have kept within that conserver of all good things.

Nothing could be more foolhardy, more dangerous, even more false — especially in a country lacking a full Catholic character — than to mark a body of political thought or program of political action as distinctively Catholic. But surely it would be also dangerous and foolhardy for us to remain mere spectators of the rising struggle for power. For in that struggle the whole Christian and humanist concept of man's nature and freedom are at stake, and the issue will determine whether the future is to hold for us, as Catholics, citizenship in a political order respecting spiritual liberty or descent anew to the catacombs.

12

THE RETURN OF THE CHURCH FROM EXILE

IN AN essay of several years ago that very thoughtful German, Peter Wust, made use of the phrase, "return of Catholicism from exile." His point was that, owing to a change come about in the intellectual atmosphere of the western world, the Church and Catholic thought had been able at last to find a place in modern culture and give their message again to the world. The dominant tendencies of thought since the atheistic eighteenth century had nearly run their course — impelled to suicidal destruction by their own inner nature — and therefore disillusionment with fallacious thinking was great enough to bring the western mind to consider again the truths of religion. Rationalism had ended in the denial of reason; naturalism had led, not to nature, but the perversion of nature; materialism had involved the denial of personality; empirical pragmatism had got the world into a chaotic mess, and so forth; wherefore had bitter experience shown the hollowness of that by which our apostate civilization has sought to live, and the way was opening for the Church 'to return from exile.'

Now, that phrase has provoked questions with which I propose to deal in this final essay. These questions are: Is this really a fact? And if it is, why has the world outside the

fold of the Faith not taken greater cognizance of so meaningful a development in twentieth-century culture?

To the average American this fact — if it be a fact — is
certainly not obvious, but rather calls for some measure of
discernment and looking below the surface of things if it
is to be seen. Ask the average man you meet if he has observed it and I doubt not he will give a negative reply. Ask
the average man who reads or even writes for the secular
press, or ask the average college professor, and although you
may get an affirmative reply, it will be something like this:
"Yes, there has been some revival of religion in the last few
years, due chiefly to the great depression, and I have heard
that quite a large number of persons have sought refuge or
emotional escape by joining the Catholic Church." The man
giving such a reply will be sure, of course, that there is
nothing much in all this, that it is just a small reaction which
might have been expected, since such things have happened
in the past, so he thinks, without halting the growth of
modern secularism and disbelief in revealed religion. If he
knows any history he may point out that romanticists, obeying emotion rather than reason, rushed back to the Church
after the French Revolution, but that they did not arrest
the progress of modern man's emancipation from religion,
or, as some prefer to put it, from dogmatic religion. No, to
the extent that such a man had noticed any strange stirring
of Catholic energies, he would be much more likely to interpret it as the twitching of a corpse rather than as the
resurrection of the dead; and the phrase, 'return of the
Church from exile,' would certainly not occur to him at all.

Now would such a person be seeing things fully and
aright? He is apparently well informed; he reads books,
even many books; he follows the reviews and goes to the
plays; he travels; he knows something of international

affairs; he is aware in a general way of the trend of things; and if he has not noticed, or but barely noticed, the resurgent vital action of the world's oldest and largest human thing, how can that resurgent action be there?

If we could call into existence another man (some wholly imaginary being), who although being a complete stranger in the world, yet would be able to view it with rational eye and disinterested desire to know it, I fancy we would find him rather puzzled by the testimony given in answer to this question. Since we postulate him as intelligent, without prejudice, and eager to learn the actual facts, we may be sure that he would seek the most reliable information available concerning the Church and its present action; that he would therefore consult some such excellent and authoritative work as, say, Michael Williams' recent volume, *The Catholic Church in Action*. In it he would come upon this statement: "Few competent observers of the trend of the age would deny and most would agree, that since the close of the World War the Catholic Church has been positively active, in a higher degree and on a broader scale than at any time since just before the Counter-Reformation. It also seems clear to many of these observers — though on this point there is less agreement — that the Catholic Church is the one great institution to escape the confusion, or threatened confusion, which has overtaken practically all the nations and states, and their forms of organization, along with the economic, political and social systems which have bound humanity together . . . during the last few centuries."[1]

Reading on in this book, which is an encyclopedic survey of the whole terrestrial action of the Church, this man would come upon a great multitude of facts that could not

---

[1] P. 2. Quoted by permission of the Macmillan Co., publishers.

but strike him as deeply significant and give pause to his mind. He would find, for one thing, that the various governments of the world are a good deal more concerned about what the Holy See does than they were a generation or two ago; the fact being evidenced by a near-tripling, since 1914, of diplomatic representatives accredited to the Vatican. He would discover also that since 1922 the mission territories of the Church had been enlarged by one third of their former size. And such facts, we may be sure, could not but give the impression of a thing energetically alive. Our imaginary man would probably be brought very swiftly to see the Church as the world's most stubbornly impressive institution, and therefore to conclude that no thinking about the future of human society can have much value if it does not posit that fact as of prime importance.

If he continued his investigations through wider fields, exploring contemporary Catholic literature, marking and comparing trends of thought within and without the Catholic fold, he would undoubtedly be struck by the vigor of the Catholic mind in breasting new fields of thought all the while it held tenaciously to the main traditions not only of western but of all human civilization. He would not at all get the impression that the Catholic mind was of the past, wholly conservative of things abandoned by the world today; it would not seem to him that this mind had insulated itself, Chinese fashion, against the outside world, content to hoard its own treasures and cherish its own traditions. No, exactly opposite would be the impression, for our inquirer would note that the Catholic mind is turned outward upon the world, is interested in all of it, feeds upon it and assimilates like a healthy organism moving in its right environment. In short, our imaginary man would be aware of the vigorous intellectual apostolate that is carried on in the world of contemporary civilization by our oldest and most conservative thing. And one may be sure he would be provoked to observe this very significant fact, that although the outside world knew rather little of the Church, the mind within the Church knew that outside world very well, very shrewdly indeed; from which it could not but follow that the mind within was of greater breadth than the mind outside.

Now having had some view of the Church as the vastly important thing that it is in world civilization of today, this inquirer would have a very good clue for understanding the history he would read in order to learn how the world came to be as he found it. That is, he would reasonably expect to find the action of this thing the main action in history; he would expect to find it in some way central to great historic crises. It would seem to him the big thing, the central thing, the very core, as it were, of history; and therefore when he read modern political and cultural history, say of the French Revolution or of the rise of liberalism, democracy, and communism — or of any of the great movements that have changed the face of western society — he would never let the Church get out of the historical picture. He would, therefore, avoid making such errors of historical interpretation as to imagine, with socialists and communists, that the central action of history is the struggle of classes for possession of the means of production; rather would he be prepared to see the struggle between the Church and its foes as the main theme of history. For he would expect to find some men always loving it more than anything else, some men always hating it more than anything else, and all men (who know it) dividing significantly according to their attitudes toward it.

What, however, he would not expect to find — and be

very puzzled to find — would be men concerned about the crisis in our civilization and yet coolly or contemptuously indifferent to this thing. That there should be persons who presume to know the world they live in and to influence it importantly, to know its history and have views as to how great problems are to be solved, and yet think little or not at all about the Church — this, we may be sure, would amaze and mystify our inquirer. Yet such men he would find, and in large numbers, in the western world today, especially in the English-speaking regions of it.

Here you have a great and unmistakable resurgence of Catholic energies: expanding missions, the attack on the social question, the revival of rational philosophy, a grappling with new moral questions arising from transformed ways of life, the enhanced prestige of the Holy See, a minimum of scandals (the vicious traducing of the clerical order in Germany to the contrary notwithstanding), a growth of conversions, and many other evidences of new Catholic life. Perhaps the most convincing is the evidence of persecution, which is carried on so bitterly in many parts of the world. There is all that going on, not secretly but openly, not as a light burning under a bushel but as one set on a hilltop. We talk and write about it, openly, sometimes even hopefully; and the world about us seems to take no notice. And by the world about us I do not mean the general run of people whose chief interests in life make little call upon their intellects and whose opinions on great matters are made for them by others. I mean rather the world of thought and learning, the world where most of the books and periodicals are produced, the world of press, school, and university, where intellectual fashions are set. Does that world know of the resurgent life of the Church today? Does it take the Church into account in its speculation about

what is today and may be tomorrow? If our imaginary inquirer moved about questioning only that world, would he
even get a hint of this formidable thing? The answer to
these questions is no. This man would be told with assurance that the Church is still what the nineteenth-century
liberal intellectuals decided it to be: a discarded garment of
western culture, a piece for the museum of history. There
would be nothing in the testimony given him to lead to
any other conclusion than that whatever the future of our
civilization is to be, the Catholic Church will have no
significant place in it. That conviction about us remains
strong, especially in America, and there should be no
blinking the fact.

There exists, indeed, what often bears the sign of a conscious conspiracy to keep that conviction firm. For consider
the near boycott of the finest Catholic literature by the
secular press, dominated as it is by Leftist intellectuals who
successfully dupe even the most conservative publishers. Or
consider the history courses and courses in contemporary
civilization mapped out and laid down by those who rule
the public secondary schools. I saw recently a ten-page syl-
labus outline of a course in modern world history for the
schools of a leading eastern state, and four of the pages
were devoted to Soviet Russia, three to the industrial and
technological developments since the eighteenth century,
and the rest to nationalism, social politics, and so forth. The
Church was not even mentioned, and there was not given
the slightest hint of the existence of a spiritual tradition in
our civilization.

But, one may ask, is not the position better in the colleges
and universities? Are not the professors who teach the
rising generation of college men and women, future leaders
of society, becoming more aware of Catholic thought, writ-

ing, and criticism? Possibly, but there are not many signs of this, and it may even be that for the moment the anti-Catholic tendency is growing stronger. There has developed in recent years, it must be remembered, a new kind of educational machinery for inculcating the belief that the Church is of no important significance in the modern world. I refer to the wide introduction of courses in the history of modern culture which simply sketch the background of our present social order. These courses are crowding the older conventional history courses, and there is in them — even though the fact be not acknowledged — the purpose of forming minds, and forming them to be anti-historical, to exalt the present and discredit the past, especially the great Christian past of western society. Everywhere there seems a tendency to sum up history in great generalizations, to skim over all that took place before the Enlightenment and the Industrial Revolution, and to interpret history in the light of values esteemed most highly by people cut loose from the great traditions of Christendom.

The fact is indicated by the increasing number of books that purport to treat of the modern western world, or of modern European civilization, as a whole; which books are demanded more and more by the colleges. Take almost any one of these, at random, and see how much treatment and what kind of treatment is given to religion, especially to the Catholic religion which for more than a thousand years was the very soul of European culture. To the extent that the book runs true to type all religion will be nearly ignored; and the author will not have had wit enough even to remark the portentous truth that this modern secular civilization, of which he treats, is the first instance in the history of the world when men have been daring enough, or better, foolhardy enough, to rest an order of society upon strictly secular principles. The books of this kind are really thoroughly anti-Catholic in tendency even where the author would be startled and chagrined to hear such a charge against his work. For if they do not treat the revolt against orthodoxy as making for freedom and progress, and if they do not treat defense of orthodoxy as obscurantism and intellectual obstinacy, then they will at least treat the opinions of the anti-Catholic more respectfully (and as having more importance) than the Catholic. To take but one example of what I mean: Karl Marx, John Stuart Mill, and John Henry Newman were almost exactly contemporary one with another in the last century, and each attained a world stature; each was great as an expounder of important and universal doctrines, and each wrote sage and penetrating observations on his times. But in the kind of books which I have here in mind, whose observations are accorded greatest respect? Perhaps Mill, perhaps Marx, but never Newman; yet the book will probably be called a history of Europe or western civilization, and Newman spoke for what was oldest, most fundamental, and most vital in our civilization. Indeed if Newman is mentioned at all it will be as a theologian, and in most of the 'new history' theologians hardly come into the picture at all.

To be quite specific I will mention two fairly recent and well-received books that fall into this general classification. About two years ago a certain Mr. Achorn published a huge work on European civilization since the French Revolution. It got a good press reception and has gained a large number of college text adoptions. It is applauded as a fine piece of that 'new history' which treats the whole cultural scene more comprehensively than the older and more narrowly political history; and students and teachers seem to like very much its spirited style and wide informative range. But

what does the author say of religion and the Church? He
tells us how obscurantist the Church was in the past century
and what sport scientists are alleged to have made of Christian doctrine; and that is about all, until he comes to the end
of his long account of everything under the sun to write
three scant pages on religion in twentieth-century culture.
Most of this is taken up by a quotation from Anatole France
who is described as "one secular writer at least (who) deserves mention in connection with religion." From this book,
which is giving hundreds of American college students their
chief information about Europe, one gets no other impression than that the Christian religion is but a historical
monument of a dead culture of the past.

Then consider the two thousand page *History of Western
Civilization* by Harry Elmer Barnes, which may be regarded
as the classic piece of this new kind of literature. It, too, has
had a successful sale and come into wide use as a book of
instruction for college students. Not only does it thoroughly
please the kind of mind that despises the past and exalts the
present, and would be prattling about the progress of civilization the night before the whole thing crashed; it has also
won high commendation from many reputable professors
whom one might have expected to snub it. As a matter of
fact, it is not without real merits: a spirited style, a considerable accuracy in factual detail, and a vast comprehensive sweep. Moreover, there is much treatment of religion,
even in the second volume which deals almost wholly with
the post-Reformation world; for Barnes is not the kind of
thinker to miss the importance of religion in history. Far
from it; he dislikes it too much to ignore it. But what does
he say of us? What view does he offer, what explanation
does he give for the vitality of Catholicism? Has he remarked its return from exile, saying, 'Here is a strange and

impressive thing: just when the general judgment of en-
lightened men was that the old thing was dead that thing
rose from the dead'? Does he marvel at the recuperative
powers of the ancient superstition, showing wonder at this
mysterious force possessed of capacity for resurrection and
counterattack upon its enemies? Of course he does nothing
of the kind, for in fact he has hardly noticed the presence
of the Church in the modern world. For him we are not as
important as Protestantism; we are but a Christian sect of
rather minor significance, of the past, a museum piece. The
man is scandalously ignorant of us, and his work bears not
the slightest indication of an awareness of modern Catholic thought. Perhaps no one has told him about us. Perhaps
he would not listen if one did tell him, I do not know. But
it is plain, that he — like most of the writers engaged in
forming the American mind today — pays no attention
whatever to the most notable works of Catholic writers in
historical scholarship, philosophy, and criticism. To his huge
history he appends a long list of specially commended books
treating generally of modern culture, and among the authors
of these one may find, in addition to Dr. Barnes himself,
such men as Wells, Russell, Walter Lippman, Harry Emer-
son Fosdick, Rexford G. Tugwell, John Dewey, Granville
Hicks, Joseph Wood Krutch, but one looks in vain for
Dawson, or Maritain, or Belloc, or Chesterton, or for any
distinguished Catholic thinker who has applied his mind to
the problems of our age. Barnes, in short, has not even a
bowing acquaintance with the modern Catholic mind.

That is the sort of blindness we are up against, even in
learned circles, in our effort to vindicate the reality of religion and the obvious palpable fact that it lives in the world
of today. These two textbook writers are not cases of ex-
traordinary myopia, but representative and characteristic

members of that class of persons in America who set and determine thought fashions; and for them the Church is dead. They are thinking about the world, probing its problems, forming and expressing judgments; but they remain children of the eighteenth and nineteenth centuries, their minds closed tight against traditional religion, still adherents to the naïve belief that our civilization can go on without the spiritual principles that informed it and constitute its soul. Our apostolate has made little headway against them.

Other barriers against us, such as communist violence and political persecution, are small as compared with this arrogant determination to treat the Church as if it were of no account. You cannot talk to people who are deaf, nor demonstrate to those who are blind; nothing but grace and miraculous conversions can surmount this wall of ignorance. We can go on with our duty of showing forth the Faith in act and word; we can pray; we can weep as our Lord wept over Jerusalem, saying with Him, "If thou hadst known, and that in this thy day, the things that are to thy peace"; but that is all we can do. The rest is with God.

Now many will say that there is nothing strange in all this; that so it has ever been; that the Church has always had to face blind arrogance, cold, haughty, contemptuous skepticism. And that is true. Our Lord certainly met with it. The Church in the early Roman Empire met with it and encountered the same kind of intellectual boycott that the modern anti-Catholic mind carries on against it. That was a main reason why the non-Catholic writers of antiquity made so few references to the thing even long after it had sprung to sturdy life thoughout the Roman world. They tell us so little about the Church that many historians have been led to believe the Church was of rather small significance in Roman life until the third century.

The answer to this is, of course, that if the intellectuals boycotted it, the politicians and magistrates (who are always closer to social reality than the intellectuals) did not boycott it, but gave it a great deal of attention by trying very hard to kill it. It is the same in our own day, and if, say five hundred years hence, a historian should endeavor to build up from non-Catholic sources alone an account of the history and position of the Church in the present-day social world, he might possibly conclude that it had then little history and less social importance. For even when violent persecution rages and men fight wars about this thing, the anti-Catholic intellectual quite commonly does not know it. Thus in Spain today he will see men fighting for power, for land, for political and economic objectives, for Fascism or Communism, but he will not see them fighting for their Faith. The real truth, of course, is not to be found in the empty reporting of the age by such bigots, but in studying the acts of politicians and magistrates. For if we would measure the force of the Church in the contemporary world, we have only to look at the efforts of State power to bring the thing under its control; the politicians are not fooled into believing it dead. If they wrote our histories, we should get a different story.

But to return to the main thought, it is quite true that the Church has always had to face this boycott and this bigoted ignorance, but that does not mean the position of forces today is not exceptional. For this kind of mentality is more completely dominant in fixing thought fashions than at any time since before the Church won its civil right to exist in the Roman empire. This mind has the schools and the press; it has political power; it commands the chief agencies of intellectual culture; it can fight us with weapons we do not possess; it can prevent us from being heard; it has all the prestige deriving from the great modern advance of secular civilization which has not yet broken into retreat; and we are nearly helpless against it. Atheism and hatred of Christ and His Church are indeed old and familiar manifestations in Christendom, but only modern times — only, indeed, the last few generations — have seen the triumph of these forces in the general cultural life of the West. They made their first open bid for power in the eighteenth century and rode to a smashing victory in the twentieth; so that we stand today, as we have not stood for fifteen centuries, in a society wherein convinced Christians and merely unthinking habitual Christians form a minority, even a persecuted minority. We no longer give flavor to society, but are rather in danger of taking flavor from it.

Now all this may seem to lead to a denial that there has been taking place any 'return of Catholicism from exile,' but it must not be so understood, since there is another side to the medal. Modern history has been, above all else, a history of the expansion of western society, the transformation of the European scene of history into a scene of world history. To a superficial observer the Church may seem to have been weakened in Europe because the clerical order has ceased to dominate society, but the Church is vastly larger and stronger throughout the world as a whole. It is battling upon a larger front and operating on new principles of campaign strategy. The relative position of forces in this larger world theater of war may be compared with the position of forces in that much smaller theater of the Roman third century, and there is neither more nor less reason to despair, or to hope for victory, in the phase of conflict now opening up, than there was in the distant days of catacomb martyrs. Actually the Church is not facing defeat today but is widening its battle line. To see the position of the present moment

rightly requires a much larger historical perspective than
can be got anywhere outside of the Church.

Moreover, in writing of ignorance, bigotry, and intellectual boycott of Catholic thought, I have been referring
primarily to the English-speaking world, and not to old
Europe, which is still the capital and center of western civilization. Peter Wust's phrase is truly descriptive of what has
been happening in many key centers of European thought,
for Europe has suffered, in the last few generations, the
ultimate consequences of heresy and atheism to an extent
that most people of the new world have not known and
probably cannot comprehend. It is therefore in the old
world that one may discern the breaking, and therefore
the recession, of the great anti-Catholic tidal wave of
modern times; it is there that one can see how much of
what is today most hostile is but the backwash of that
broken wave.

A summary view of the last century surely indicates that
this is so. The eighteenth century in which, as it has been
said, the anti-Christian forces made their first open bid for
power, was a century of social decay ending in a revolutionary upheaval that affected ultimately every part of
Europe and shattered an old order of life in which Catholicism had been so deeply intertwined that very many
persons identified the Faith with that old order. Wherefore
it was believed that the Faith too would pass away, and this
confidence in its passing was accompanied by a high optimism about the future of a human race set free from
tyrants and priests.

This was the age of Romanticism, a movement charged
with unrest and revolt. During its ascendancy the currents
of thought and doctrine swirled and crossed one another,
so that it was hard to determine what way the mind of

Christendom was actually taking. On the one hand, this spirit was allied with liberalism and that optimistic vision of a coming glorious human liberty. But on the other hand, it was in part a revolt against the Revolution itself; that is, it had also a reactionary character which was revealed to the extent that men became disillusioned with the results of the Revolution. Sentiment reacted against a rationalism which in practice seemed rather to lay waste than to renew the face of the world, and there appeared a disposition to idealize older times, especially to conjure up a vision of the Middle Ages as a golden time for humanity. That is one reason why a Catholic revival took place at this time. But there was no great substance in this romanticist Catholicism, for too many men were equating Catholicism with medievalism, which is a very wrong equation. Moreover, the romanticist mind turned to the old religion as a thing of rich beauty and spiritual luxury, rather than as a thing rational, dogmatic, and objectively true; so that it seems fair to say that the romanticist Catholicism of a century ago was not really a strong protest against the movement of the western mind away from the Church.

Now, in the second half of the nineteenth century a distinct change in the intellectual climate became manifest. Romantic revolution quieted down; not so ardently did men throw themselves into remaking the world in the spirit of Byron, Shelley, Mazzini, and Fichte. In philosophy subjectivist idealism, so characteristically romantic, went down before positivism, atheistic rationalism, and scientific materialism. Irreligion spread more widely. Industrialism and all the deceptive prosperity that it can create increased, and the dreams of the great revolutionaries began to be discredited almost as much as the old order against which the Revolution had been thrown. The western world seemed to be settling down to a smug, middle-class and philistine comfort, ignoring religion more than persecuting it, content not to raise ultimate human questions at all. Science and mechanism colored thought and interest, wealth increased, and the old revolutionary optimism for a world made free passed into a more stupid optimism for evolving, through science and technology, a world of wealth and leisure. The life of the spirit flagged, and even the revolutionaries passed from romantic and humanitarian socialism, with its appeal to justice and the rights of man, to Marxian socialism with its pseudoscientific and materialist premises. The general atmosphere of the period was suffocating for really Catholic-minded human beings, who passed upon it a condemnation more severe than any denunciation uttered by socialist revolutionaries. Perhaps in the whole history of Christendom there was never a time when all values were so near to being computed in pounds, shillings, and pence.

Inevitably, optimism began at length to fail, and one heard instead the opposite note of pessimism sounded more and more distinctly in European thought and literature. The old world, by the end of the century, was showing signs of deep disillusionment and spiritual thirst; grave matters were being pondered, and the mind was turning again to questions having to do with the ends of human life. The great secular civilization, the life of wealth and comfort, of industrial capitalism, of impressive scientific achievement — what was it for? How could it achieve any final and worth-while consummation of man? What was man anyway? A bit of chemistry? A clever animal? A mere biological accident in a purposeless world of nature? These were the questions pressing forward again, and the fact was pregnant of meaning. Millions felt the pressure, hardly knowing why, but proving that their souls were troubled by the frantic effort to escape from pessimism in frenzied nationalism, social reform, and at length the Great War.

All this was apparent by 1914, and the sign of the times indicated that a revival of religion, or at least of the religious spirit, was under way. The form this would take might, of course, be some new heresy even more mad than the old ones which were dying; and this we have seen come to pass in Marxian Communism and the insane German religion of blood and race. But to the extent that it would be Christian and traditionalist it was certain to be Catholic, since Protestantism was in open and acknowledged decay. Unlike Catholicism it had not been sent into exile, but had remained to disintegrate with the world of strict secularism. It was crippled by attacks from within its own body; it was in open retreat from its own once defended dogmas and even from essential affirmations of universal Christian acceptance. Watered down, diluted by compromise with hostile elements, there was no adequate reason for expecting it to gain any new lease of strong life (at least where thinking is rigorous), even though the western mind was turning again in search of spiritual reality.

Altogether different was the position of the old Church. It was not in retreat from its dogmas, but was excommunicating, as of old, the heretics who denied them; it was not watered down, but was whole and what it had always been. When the world had rejected it, it had made no offer of compromise, nor pleaded to be taken along on the wild joy ride to what Pius IX called "progress, liberalism, and civilization, as lately introduced." It had resolutely remained itself and where it had always been;

so that it was there to be found again by men after they had stumbled through the long darkness.

Wherefore did it come about that the scales were dropping from blinded eyes. The revival of rational philosophy proceeded at accelerated pace, and some of the subtlest minds were formed to receive the Faith. Grace touched the souls of men who learned humility, and moreover, that passionate interest in the social question (which showed that even in our lapsed faith we had not wholly ceased to be the sons of Christendom) turned attention to the fact that the Church had really been pioneer in this field and stood for a co-operative and corporative individualism that denied the bankrupt liberalism on the one hand and the menacing socialist advance on the other. All this and more, by 1914, had come as witness to Catholic revival, and everybody who really knew the inner life of the age knew that the Church might become again the spiritual mistress of western society; certainly few intelligent persons any longer believed the Church destined for the museum. That trend is infinitely stronger today, with recognition growing ever more clear that the Church in communion with Rome is the mainstay of reason, order, and justice in the secularized and barbarized society of European nations.

It is this return to reason and reality, this spiritual and intellectual movement manifesting itself in the old world, that should inspire some measure of optimism and hope for new victories of the Faith in our own world in the years lying not far beyond today. The spiritual manifestations of Europe invariably impregnate also the new world, for our culture fundamentally is all one. And the proof is plain that the deeper currents of the age are flowing favorably to great Catholic progress here. Also, it must be remembered that movements of the spirit go with great speed today, and none can tell but that a great miracle of grace may be vouchsafed. And finally we must recognize, as Christopher Dawson has shrewdly pointed out, that "current beliefs are always out of date. It is difficult to realize how much current thinking belongs to the past, because it is natural for men's minds to be soaked in the mental atmosphere of the last generation, and it needs a considerable effort to see things as they are and not as other people have seen them. The artist and the philosopher and the scientist, each in his own way, see life direct, but the majority of men see it secondhand through the accepted ideas of their society and culture. And consequently, the tendencies that we regard as characteristic of the age are often those which were characteristic of the age that is passing rather than of that which is beginning." These facts should fortify our hopes.